COUNTRY LIVIN'

Two City Teens Work a Summer on the Farm

The Farms of Washington County, Pennsylvania

ANDREW STEVANS

Sketches by Madeline Bowden

D1512209

Country Livin'
Two City Teens Work a Summer on the Farm
© Andrew L. Stevans 2012

ISBN: 978-0-9848340-1-3
Library of Congress Control
Number: 2012903168

Twelve essays in this book
were previously published in the
Pittsburgh Post Gazette

For Information Contact
P.O. Box 613
Merrifield, VA 22116-0613

-BOOK EDITION-

Printed in the USA
CreateSpace

7290 Investment Drive, Suite B
North Charleston, SC 29418

THE FARM: PETERS TOWNSHIP
WASHINGTON COUNTY, PA

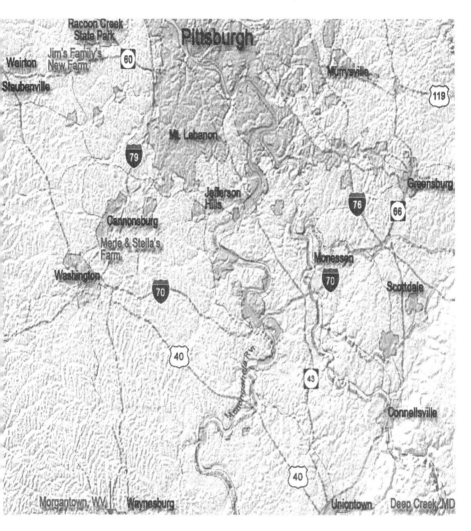

CONTENTS

FALL...

AFTERWARDS

ACKNOWLEDGEMENTS

COUNTRY LIVIN' (from the back cover)

Two City Teens' work a Summer on the Farm

RED'S BEST SHOT... Merle suddenly yelled to the retriever, "Red, put the chickens to bed!" Red seemed startled at first. He could only raise one ear and it was raised high. Then he took off, up the path toward the chicken house, barking and carrying on. The gangly retriever could actually climb trees.

WALLY RIDER... Wally appeared small for his six years. But his mind was as quick as a cat's, his chatter as fast as a scared monkey's. What he couldn't do with his hands and feet, he coaxed out of the old car with threat and innuendo.

CORNTEST... Jim raked the first cob clean with one motion. "There's no hurry, Jim". "Hungry," he said, quickly cleaning a second cob. I consoled myself with the thought that his teeth were bigger than mine. I methodically crunched row after row.

CHAWIN' HABIT... I memorized the easy way the farmer's fingers grasped and measured the chaw. I took a fresh wad. He showed me how to hold it in my cheek, up high. I didn't like the sharp tobacco taste, but the thought of long spits and deadly accuracy drove me on.

BOW HUNTING... The rabbit took a hop. Its front legs pawed the air. Then it moved about a foot, then another. Could I have pinned it through the tail? That's impossible, I thought. But my arrow disappeared into the underbrush.

Andy Stevans

Andrew Stevans grew up in Pittsburgh Pennsylvania. He has worked as a farm hand, a Navy non-com, an IBM engineer, an adult-ed teacher, and an HR manager. He now lives in Northern Virginia.

INTRODUCTION

THINGS YOU OUGHT TO KNOW...

What follows in *Country Livin'* are true-life stories of farm life as seen through the eyes of a 13-year-old, city of Pittsburgh teen. But this teen, new to farm life, is trying to keep up with a 17-year old neighbor who had worked on the farm the previous summer and "knows the ropes."

The farms are located in Peters Township, Washington County, Pennsylvania--the fertile farm belt just south of the city of Pittsburgh. Some of the small, family-owned farms in that region still operate. The farmers' hard-working, fun-loving way-of-life continues to this day.

In general, this is nonfiction, and to the best of my memory, the way events happened. A dozen of the stories appeared in the Sunday *Pittsburgh Post Gazette's* wide area edition (*Washington, Mid-Mon Valley & Greene Counties*). Merle and Stella, and other local farm folk recalled and found joy in the episodes related.

Merle and Stella or Merle's brother, Ray, may have owned a camera, but few photos have survived. Several are found in the Afterwards of Country Livin'.

My hope is that, upon reading *Country Livin'*, you experience the feelings of exhilaration and joy, and the pangs of pain and sadness as I did. All else is unintentional.

The Author

Courtesy of Jim Hacker

...SPRING...

Courtesy of Madeline Bowden

WASHINGTON COUNTY

The farm belt and Washington County, Pennsylvania were new to me. Jim, a neighbor, had worked as a farm hand on Merle and Stella's farm the previous summer. He asked me to take his place.

Jim would be joining his family on their newly purchased farm, in the next county, later that summer. We sat at the back of a Pittsburgh Greyhound bus that would wind its way

1

through the Liberty Tunnel and south to McMurray in about an hour. Jim started complaining about feeling sick. Just as the bus pulled up to the McMurray stop, his loud belch turned heads.

"We're here. Let's go quick."

Jim was a family friend, 17 years old, husky, and over six-feet. I was barely 14 and much smaller, struggling with two brown, double-thick shopping bags full of clothes. Jim said it was a several mile hike to the farm, and I was wondering if I would make it.

We walked at least a mile in the cool morning air. From time to time, Jim staggered complaining of stomach pains. He finally took one of my bags of clothes, "To help you out, I'll try to carry this bag to that large tree near Dutch's hill, up ahead."

Jim pointed to a tree on the side of the road, at least a half-mile down the macadam. In spite of Jim's sickness, he kept me entertained with local farm stories, and even tried to scare me with a story about Merle's cantankerous cow, Connie.

The day was warming up. A network of gnats adopted us and each time we slowed they began their endless darting about our heads. A distant hill, spotted with cattle, loomed directly ahead.

"That entire hill belongs to Dutch's farm," Jim said. "There are only two more miles to Merle and Stella's."

Jim talked on. He told of Merle's skill with a baseball. Merle had played in the farm leagues in Washington County, and Jim felt he could have been a great pitcher. But, like Jim, Merle loved farm work.

The road seemed to stretch on forever. Finally, we reached the base of Dutch's hill. Jim handed me my bag and held his stomach. He half fell, half sat down under the tree.

"Follow the road around the hill. On the other side, you'll see the reddog to the left."

I stood quietly, studying Jim, awaiting further instructions.

"Does the red dog belong to a farmer?" Jim scratched his head in disbelief.

"Reddog is gravel. Merle's farm is about a mile down the reddog road. Now go!"

Jim appeared a lot sicker, belching and moaning, leaning back against the tree. Gathering the bags, I staggered at a quicker gait.

It seemed that I had completely circled Dutch's hill when I spotted the reddog. A car was coming up fast, spewing endless trails of red dust. I decided to rest a moment on the shoulder of the highway to avoid breathing the dirt-filled air. The vehicle spun and came to a halt near me. Jim and another man were inside.

My mouth dropped open. Jim had on his biggest smile.

"Let me introduce you to Merle. We'll be working for him." I was dumfounded.

"Jim, you were sick two miles back. What happened?" I said.

Seeing my disbelief, Jim's grin got wider. He had taken a short-cut over Dutch's hill.

Too tired to get angry, I shook Merle's hand and let Jim help me load the bags into the car.

Merle drove the road like a racetrack. On curves, the rear tires skewed in the loose gravel, sliding the car sideways.

"Don't worry young fella. We'll be there in a minute."
Merle caught my eye in his rear-view mirror.
Jim was sitting next to Merle. He wasn't saying much. I
noticed he was wedged into the seat, holding on to the back of
Merle's seat with one hand and pressing against the door-
frame with the other.
We entered a long driveway that ended at a barn. Merle
jumped out of the car motioning to me to come around. He
introduced me to Stella, a smiling, dark-haired lady whom I
liked at once.
"Lunch will be on the table in ten minutes," she
announced. "Jim, you show your friend around the farm—and
don't be late for lunch."
"Late, for lunch?" Jim said in disbelief. "Who, me?" We
all laughed. Obviously, they also knew about Jim's appetite.

Jim provided a short tour of the farm. I was ushered
quickly through the chicken houses, past the barn and by a
large pig pen—the smell was overwhelming. We took a
moment to pet the old hound, Mitzi. Jim explained that she
was Merle's famous retired pheasant dog, known throughout
Washington County.

Following lunch, Jim and I spent the afternoon picking
green beans, cucumbers and tomatoes for Saturday's sale at
the South Side Pittsburgh Farmers' Market.
Shortly after dinner, Jim and I fed the few hundred
chickens and collected eggs. We then joined Merle at the barn
where he demonstrated how to place a leather belt, figure-
eight fashion, around the back legs of Connie, his
cantankerous cow.

"That will be your job from now on, young fella. But, be careful, or Connie will kick you flat."

I'm sure I looked alarmed. Merle winked at Jim, chuckled, and threw me a catcher's mitt.

"We're going to let the electric vacuum milking system do the milking chore," he said. I watched the methodical movement of the stainless steel tubes Merle had attached to Connie. I could hear the freshly drawn milk begin hitting the bottom of the empty bucket in a rhythmic beat.

"Every ten minutes we'll switch to another cow." Merle explained. "And for the next thirty minutes, we're going to throw the ball. Let's go, boys."

Somewhat later, I lay in bed trying to comprehend the country night. I remember extending my hand into its velvet blackness and seeing nothing.

QUIRKS

Merle had four cows. He said he would not own a bull. Merle didn't trust the unpredictable nature of bulls. I heard many harsh tales about bulls' antics from Merle. He had heard them from Big Bill "Bull" O'Brian, a neighbor who had raised bulls all his life. That summer I learned a few frightening lessons about animals that I could never forget; lessons about their excellent memories, and their unpredictability.

Before my excursion into the country, I was aware that cats and dogs had their own personalities. But I had no idea that all animals had their "quirks." Some carried on to the point where I began to suspect they were human.

Merle had names for many of his animals. Suzie was quiet and attractive for a cow, a Guernsey that looked like she had recently walked out of a Borden Dairy commercial. Connie was a Holstein. She provided most of the milk and had the worst disposition. The other two cows pretty much just blended in, providing their modicum of milk—and an occasional quirk.

Calf—we called her that because Merle only had the one—was a gentle, alert animal. Cat—the crazy kitten with one eye—was born within hours of Calf in the same stall. They'd buddy around, as amazing as that sounds. Calf would always watch not to step on Cat. But that's another story.

Merle had six pigs—unnamed, smelly, and in all respects just routine, big, noisy, lazy pigs, waiting for the inevitable. But Ray, Merle's brother, had a twenty-acre fenced-in pig orchard full of apple trees and half-wild, ornery, black pigs. They ate everything from apples to snakes. Ray said they loved snakes.

Relatively speaking, you could do no wrong if you fed them apples. They'd fight, bite, and ram each other in a feeding frenzy. In all respects, they had the manners of pigs. The safest place for the conservative feeder was well up an apple tree or outside the pig orchard fence.

MERLE

Merle was an enigma. Pensive, not moody, he possessed a good sense of humor. Merle was kind and caring, yet, when he worked, he did so with a vengeance. I concluded that work helped him forget some bitter memories, perhaps of close friends or family lost in the wars. He spoke occasionally of war. He explained that a set of congenital bad nerves and a stammer kept him out of the action. Some years later, Merle would be one of the few to be run over by a tractor and live to tell about it.

Merle played baseball in the farm leagues around Washington County. Jim said Merle was well on his way to playing minor league ball. His dream was to pitch against a major league team.

Each evening, Merle brought out the mitts and we threw the ball. I think he could have made it in baseball. He had concentration.

"His real love is farming," Stella said. "At least he isn't wounded or worse, like some of our friends and family who were in the war."

FRIENDS

Jim had gone over to Ray's farm, about a half-mile down the reddog, to help out for the day. He returned about an hour before dinner, vaulting up the front steps toward the kitchen, and waving to me in the vegetable garden.

"I'm going to clean up for supper. Don't work too hard." The screen door slammed behind him before I could answer.

I continued to hoe for another five minutes and took a break. Merle approached from the barn. I sat watching a dozen or so kittens playing, while petting one of them. Shaking his head at my fascination with the animals, he winked and squatted down, reaching to pet a tiger stripe.

"You came all the way out here to make friends?" Merle seemed incredulous. He removed his baseball cap and wiped his face in one practiced motion. A hint of mischief played around his eyes.

"Well, let's see, there are 300 chickens, minus seven roosters each week for market; there's 20 ducks and a couple

11

broods—what the rats and snappers and hawks don't get; and there's six geese, but I wouldn't get too close to them—one broke Stella's finger."

I tried to interrupt, but Merle was caught up in his thinking and went on. "There's a bunch of cats—half of them are wild, and 17 kittens; two dogs—but they're loyal to one master except for the pup; ground hogs, squirrels, dozens of rats and mice. And there must be a thousand per acre of bees, wasps, hornets, and yellow jackets, and spiders, flees, and ticks—and God knows what else is out there. Take your pick."

He chuckled, adjusted the bill on his cap down over his eyes with finality, and started to walk toward the house. "And hell, say howdy for me if you get to know some real good."

Merle may have really been telling me to get back to work. I had one row left to hoe, and Stella had just given the five-minute call for supper. I returned to my hoeing. The day passed too quickly.

Courtesy of Madeline Bowden

RED'S BEST SHOT

Merle had three dogs. In addition to old Mitzi and her pup, there was a young retriever named Red. I didn't know Red's function. He'd bark at strangers, occasionally at us, and chase the geese until they chased him. That was about it.

Merle trained many of his dogs to flush out pheasants, a favorite pastime in Washington County. He tried to explain to me that dogs often train themselves. Then, one day, I saw what Red had taught himself.

13

As usual, one evening Merle was sitting on the porch step petting Red. We could see the chickens nesting on the ground in the chicken yard. Some had started to roost in the trees. Merle wouldn't allow the chickens to roost outside the chicken house.

"They're open to any predator and they'll start layin' eggs everywhere," he said.

Suddenly, he commanded Red: "Put the chickens to bed. Go on, Red. Put the chickens to bed."

Red seemed startled at first. He could only raise one ear and it was raised high. Then he took off, up the path toward the chicken house, barking and carrying on.

The gangly, large retriever could actually climb trees. He jumped up and out onto the lower limbs to chase the roosting chickens. The squabbling was intense. Never had I seen so many cubic feet of airborne feathers.

From the back of the chicken yard appeared a white bantam rooster. He was buying none of Red's action. With hysterical clucking, his wings flapping, he half walked, half flew across the yard at Red.

Red ran for dear life, down the path toward Merle. Then, realizing that he hadn't completed his task, he returned to face off with the rooster. Red was determined to give it his best shot. But he was chased away a second and a third time. He seemed desperate. Merle ignored him.

Most of the chickens had made it into the chicken house, and finally the feisty rooster ran up into the house to join the hens. Red walked toward the porch but stopped halfway. He

14

raised his one ear, studied Merle for a moment, then slowly turned toward the barn. With his tail down and his head drooping, he went to his shed. He wouldn't look at Merle. All Merle's coaxing couldn't bring Red back to the porch.

THINNING RATS

The days wore pleasantly on. Jim appeared anxious to leave to join his family on their newly acquired farm near Raccoon State Park in the adjoining county. He and Merle could be found engrossed in conversations about strawberry farming, seasonal changes, and adverse weather for planting, growing, and harvesting. I had to hand it to Jim; he wanted to memorize every fact about farming and farm life.

Jim also had an enthusiasm for teaching me about all facets of farm life, particularly if it allowed him the chance to demonstrate his skills. It was following one of his conversations with Merle that he mentioned that rats were cunning and vicious.

I knew he was warming up to a favorite subject.

"But, they've got to eat," he said. "Pig and cow meal is a favorite of theirs—so, why don't we hunt some rats down at the barn?"

We walked single-file inside and to the back of the barn. Jim lifted up one of the large feed-bin doors. Inside were a couple hundred pounds of cow feed. Jim said that the other bin was full of pig feed. A locust rail ran along the front of the two feed bins and a hundred-watt light bulb hung overhead. Jim flipped on the light to check for rat tracks or droppings in the feed. He pointed to the loft above.

"These suckers come from up there and also from the spring out back. They'll usually run along this locust rail to get to the feed bins. They're only active at night, so you don't see them during the day."

"But what will Merle think if we shoot up his barn, Jim?"

"Merle's as concerned about the rats as anyone," Jim explained. "Rats eat their weight in feed every day, and they cause a lot of damage. Merle's worried about them gnawing through the overhead air hoses for the milking system. The cats get some of them, but rats are cunning and tough; sometimes it can take several cats to kill one rat." Jim smiled an evil smile. "Sometimes the cats need help with thinning rats. These hollow-point shells won't go through most of this wood around here anyway," Jim went on, impressed with himself. "But, man, when they hit a rat, it's goodbye Charlie. The shells will expand on impact, and blow 'em away."

I had seen what a hollow-point, 22-long bullet could do to a groundhog poking its head out of its hole. I was convinced.

That night and the next night we left the feed bin light on. By week's end we knew they'd visited. Jim pointed into the bin. "Tracks and droppings in the feed." He was pleased and I was anxious.

The moon was full that evening, bathing the yard and barn in luminescent glow. We sat on a hillside about thirty yards from the open barn door. The feed bins were easily visible through the doors.

Jim spotted the first movement through his scope. We held back as several large, king rats paraded across the locust rail. Hiding outside the barn with the door open, our gunfire wouldn't scare the cows or arouse the rats' suspicions.

In one hour, we'd killed a dozen rats. Even as one rat dropped, the one behind ignored the carcass and continued toward its goal—the feed bins. The rats were wary and alert, but they couldn't connect the shooting from outside with their dilemma inside.

Each day we cleaned up bodies and each night we shot more rats. I'm sure that we had gone through a couple of generations. As rats crossed the rail, Jim shot, using his 6-power scope. If I missed with my single shot, he backed me up.

Some of the shots must have ricocheted up and under the feed-bin covers. When Merle started finding spent 22 caliber hollow-point lead in the feed, he stopped our fun. By then, it didn't matter. Thinning rats had lost our interest.

NEW BUICK

It was the day after the storm. The creek ran swollen all that Saturday. Stella and Merle had spent the day at the South Side Farmer's Market. My first week at the farm was coming too quickly to an end.

Stella returned from the South Side Market alone in the truck. Shortly after, Merle arrived in a new Buick. He had that proud, possessive air of new ownership, a complete preoccupation with all the car's bells and whistles. Windows were being checked—up and down, the trunk lid flew open, lights were on high beam, then low—Merle said he was trying to check the light levels against the side of the barn. All that we could see was a barn lit by the rays of a setting sun. Windshield wipers started up. Like a magician, Merle suddenly appeared under the hood checking fluid levels and tapping his foot to the blaring radio.

Earlier, Jim and I had remained at the farm to do milking and clean the chicken houses. Late Friday evening, I had performed what became one of my favorite tasks. I had churned butter using an old, wooden country churner. Of course, I had helped myself to some of the buttermilk that had collected around the butter. After commenting to Jim that it wasn't thick like city buttermilk and that the stuff tasted bad, Jim downed a small glass and wiped his face. "It's what made me grow," he said, almost under his breath. He smiled encouragement.

All Saturday, I had the runs. But we were asked to take a spin with Merle in the new car so I got into the back seat.

"Let's see what this baby can do," Merle mumbled, more to himself than to us. We were off, spinning a half-turn in the mud driveway, climbing up to sixty miles per hour on the reddog gravel. The rear end of the Buick skewed to the right and left finding the outside parameters of the gravel road several times before we hit the black top highway.

"Now we're going to open her up," said Merle, winking at Jim and glancing back at me. It was almost dark. We had to be doing a hundred. I was scared and lay down on the seat. Jim looked scared too but acted relaxed, his one arm draped over the seat. That's when I smelled the odor coming from Jim's front side of the car. Merle announced that the Buick was doing a hundred miles an hour. The car swallowed curves like it was on a race track. He turned to Jim. "What the hell's that smell?"

Jim, a sick bravado painted on his face, explained to Merle that I was scared, "He's had the runs all day; probably has it all over the back of your car."

"What…?" I started. Jim glanced back at me nervously and winked.

"You wait," Merle stammered, "we'll stop at the bowling alley just up here in Canonsburg."

We did. It was an uneventful ride back to the farm.

HORNET KILLER

Jim was big and impressionable. His moods could fluctuate from kind, benevolent friend and philosophical mentor to non-communicative or even combative adversary.

It was about midday. Jim and I were near the barn, knocking mud off the tractor. The hornets seemed extra curious. Maybe it was the smell of the soft, partially dried mud on the tractor tires.

Hornet's nests are as much a part of barns as are cats, field rats, and farm animals. Merle's hornets were concentrated in a tractor storage area, built into the side of the barn. Field tools—attachments for plowing and cultivating—an old horse yoke, and several pitch forks were stored there.

Many small hornets' nests were along the top of the storage area door. Other nests, looking like immense, one-level bee hives, spread on the walls near the same entrance.

They were ominous just by their size and they spread several hand lengths at the head-ducking level.

Hornets and wasps have an affinity for mud. The pig yard and a stream beyond provided the attraction. Jim said he hated hornets and they knew it. I knew Jim was up to something.

The hornet's nests were easy to see at the front entrance. But if you weren't thinking as you parked the tractor, your head could brush against them. I wondered aloud why there were so few larger nests. Jim said that it was his job to keep them small.

"I keep their population down," Jim answered confidently. He picked up a long, slender pole. "I keep this around. It's a hornet killer." Jim flipped the seven-foot pole from hand to hand.

We hid around the corner of the barn, out of sight of the hornets. Using the pole, Jim tried to knock down the smaller nests by rubbing them off at their points of contact. After the nest was on the ground, we would let it lie for a moment or two until the frenzied hornets disbursed. Then he or I swiftly crushed them with our boot to kill any of the remaining unwary occupants.

Using his hornet killer, Jim would flatten the larger nests with powerful swatting motions against the barn wall. The hornets' fury was obvious. They'd dart at almost invisible speed, looking for an intruder. They would light on the end of Jim's pole and strut around. I never thought to check the wood for stinger marks. After all, the hornets had to vent their rage on something. Jim was merciless.

Merle came by the barn. "What the hell are you stirring them up for, Jim?" Merle fearlessly ducked into the barn storage area and took a hand-pump spray can from behind the seat of the old tractor. He sprayed each nest a few times, put the can back on the tractor, and walked over to where we were standing.

"Merle's spraying water on their wings so that they can't fly away," Jim explained. "Now I can really get them with this hornet killer."

Merle winked at Jim with a chuckle. "Yep, special water I run in the tractor." Merle continued walking up toward the house. "You boys coming to lunch?" he asked, still smiling.

"Oh, and Jim, make sure Stella gets her killer clothesline pole back." Merle chuckled again. I laughed at Jim holding Stella's clothes pole so menacingly.

I smelled gasoline as Merle's spraying worked its way down the side of the barn. Jim explained that Merle must have accidentally used gasoline to spray the hornets. "That'll probably kill 'em, too," he mused.

I ran to catch up with Merle. Jim was far behind, running awkwardly with the clothesline pole.

"There's a hornet on your shoulder," he yelled. "Let me get it with my hornet killer."

RABBITS AND PYTHAGORAS

$\mathbf{A}$ few days later, a Friday afternoon, several of the local farmers, Merle, Jim and I were in the fields behind Merle's. Everyone was taking a short break, awaiting a tractor. There were intermittent summer breezes, as clouds skated across the threatening sky, a brief respite from the hot sun. Someone was commenting on the agility of chickens.

Nothing except maybe a chicken changes direction as fast as a rabbit. Some people think that you can easily catch a chicken in an open area. It's very difficult.

But everybody knows that catching a rabbit, anywhere, is impossible, in fact, foolhardy. Rabbits are evasive and fast on any terrain. That's inherent knowledge from childhood.

Playing sandlot football back home, I was always the fastest runner on the team. Jim was always the biggest on either team. Jim had told Merle about my speed.

It was Merle who spotted the small rabbit in the field, far from any shelter. Merle winked at me and commented, "Ray's little boy Wally could catch that rabbit with his bare hands. Can you?"

I definitely was on the spot. Everyone smiled encouragement. Jim assured them that I could do it—that I had speed. He massaged my shoulders and arms. Then he smacked me on the rump in true jock fashion. He was no help.

Off I went, stalking, jogging, stalking. I was losing my audience. Merle yelled, "You gotta chase it down. It won't let you pet it. Let's get back to work."

The challenge was out. I went full speed. The men seemed awed. The rabbit would dart, I would dart; it would fade to the right, and go to the left, I faded to the right and went to the left.

With diminishing strength, I realized that by smoothing out all the darts and fades, I could cut across center and save energy. It would be a few more years before I learned the Pythagorean Theorem in geometry, but that day I learned the value of cutting corners.

Without warning, the small exhausted animal stopped dead in its tracks. A roar of approval went up along with peals of laughter as I almost tripped over the statue-like rabbit. I had run it down.

I felt pretty good for the remainder of that short, rainy work day.

CRICKET

On one hot summer's evening,
As I approached the Farm house door,
I didn't sense his watching,
Nor saw his leap—nor that he'd leapt once more.

He saw me, I know he did,
Then he leapt beneath my shoe.
What could I do but what I did?
Now there lies, free of soul, his residue.

I feel no remorse within me.
How could I have re-acted otherwise?
What caused him not to flee,
But, instead, to pit his tiny self against my size.

Yet, here I sit to further ponder,
Since I've caused his sad demise.
Perhaps he now feels he's the larger,
As he views tiny me from in the sky.

...SUMMER...

Summer came on hot, sweaty hot, unbearably hot. At least that's what the farmers were saying. On the other hand, I didn't seem to feel the heat. And the nights were usually cool and breezy...

UNDERSTANDING RATS

It was in the wee hours of the morning. The old hound Mitzi had something cornered down by the barn. Jim awoke mumbling that it was probably a field rat. They lived at the back of the barn near the pig pens and down in the creek.

I had never personally seen a rat. Grabbing Merle's flashlight, I ran toward the barks and yips, worried about the wisdom of old Mitzi's maneuver. Jim was busy at the house loading his rifle.

Maybe a rat got some of her pups once, I thought. Then I saw Mitzi, her hind legs and tail waving me over. As I approached, I played the flashlight along the bottom of the barn and near the pig fence. Rats are cunning and could be

31

vicious. "They'll go for a man's throat when cornered," Jim had warned.

I was not prepared when the light reflected from two demon-red eyes. The large rodent seemed to dare me. It didn't try to run, but stood defiantly on its hind legs staring into the light. Hate and instinct took over. My hand found a piece of wood somewhat longer than a baseball bat. The rat sensed danger but not in time. The wood hit it square. I struck at it again and again.

Mitzi lost interest. I leaned against the pig fence, shaking. Jim stood silently watching, his loaded rifle hanging from his hand.

The next morning, Jim related the story to Merle and Stella. "That rat had plenty of time to make its escape," I said, shaking my head and trying not to recall the demon eyes. Merle said he never understood rats.

Courtesy of Madeline Bowden

WALLY RIDER

I frequently enjoyed the company of Wally, Merle's young nephew and was entertained by his acting up. Wally appeared small for his six years. But he was faster than a speeding bullet in thought, word, and action. He could leap tall milk cans in a single bound. Little Wally was one of a kind. Even his way of walking was his own. He swaggered with a pronounced gait that reminded me of a miniature sailor still on his sea legs.

33

Wally was the best young equipment operator I have known. His ability to field ride a tractor or car, his knowledge and timing on steep grades and his skill at knowing where not to go were awe-inspiring.

Anything that Wally undertook had to be done at top speed. His sense of balance and motion was born in him, but what he couldn't do with his hands and feet, he coaxed out of the equipment with threats and innuendo.

Wally's mind was as quick as a cat's, his chatter as fast as a scared monkey's. Half the time he ended up talking to himself because we couldn't follow his train of thought.

There are many memories of young Wally, but one that stands out is what I call the Wally-Rider.

That particular day, Wally asked me to walk with him to pick up the old Ford out in the fields. The car, which was used to take tools and equipment to the thresher crews, had to be brought back to the farm around the pig orchard.

At some point over the years, the keys had been misplaced or lost. Ray, Wally's father, had taught Wally how to hot-wire the car. As Wally played with the wires, he talked a mumbo-jumbo that I couldn't follow. Suddenly, the old car shuddered to life.

With the car bucking, Wally rolled the left front tire out of an immense dry hole as deftly as one would spin onto a highway from a shoulder. I congratulated him on his skill.

"Any fool could do that!" I barely understood him. I managed to suppress a grin.

His head and eyes would pop up, peeping between the steering wheel and the dash, then his entire body would slide down to the floor boards to change gears. Like a small circus performer in center ring, he entertained me with his strength and skill, guiding the lumbering vehicle with precision around the trees.

At the end of the orchard was a wide gravel ramp. I jumped out to unfasten the wire gate and glanced through the window of the oncoming old Ford.

At first, the vehicle appeared empty. Then suddenly, as Wally finished his downward slide to hit the brake pedal, his head and eyes popped up over the dash. The car lurched by and I re-hitched the gate.

Near the base of the gravel ramp, the car's front end dropped sharply. The left front wheel had found another deep, dry hole. There was some frantic motion inside as the engine died. Wally couldn't get the car restarted.

The door opened, almost magically. I couldn't see little Wally. Suddenly, he was on the ground, looking even smaller against the car's awkward position. I assured him that he had done his best. He hitched up his pants giving me a sidelong glance, and said, "Let's go eat. I'll get it out after supper."

We were almost to the porch when he turned to me. Grabbing my arm, he looked up, his eyes pleading, "Don't tell a soul about that car, or I'll never live it down."

PIG ORCHARD

It was late June. Jim had shown me a short-cut through the pig orchard to Ray's house. Jim convinced me that this was a good short-cut. Not only did it save walking around Merle and Stella's house, and then down Venetia Road, but you could eat apples most of the way to Ray's. Instead of walking on gravel for a quarter-mile, it was easier to hike across Merle's cucumber patch for a couple of hundred yards, hop the pig fence, and continue to follow the road through Ray's apple orchard, while evading his half-wild pigs. The evasion part was the challenge and the real attraction.

It is an unsettling experience to have a band of wildly squealing pigs charge directly at you. I knew that pigs would bite as viciously as mad dogs. I'd climb an apple tree to get away from them.

Ray had at least thirty pigs. He gave them jurisdiction over a 15-acre, fenced-in apple orchard. When the apples were ripe and falling, it was definitely pig heaven. But usually the pigs appeared hungry. The wide open space made them a little wild.

And they moved fast; looking and sounding like an awkward herd of half-crazed buffalo, they'd surround my tree. I would watch them fighting each other for position, waiting for something or someone to fall out.

If I didn't throw them apples, they'd soon lose interest and wander off. But I developed a new game. Throwing many apples a distance from the tree, I would scramble to the ground to see how far I could sprint before I'd have to climb again.

I was good at running and climbing. Aside from my perceived danger, the pigs were getting a piece of the action and actually seemed to enjoy the game.

Late one morning, I was treed well into the orchard, about forty yards from Merle's side of the orchard fence. Ray's precocious, six-year-old son Wally, attracted by the noise, climbed into the pig orchard to join me.

"Stay back, Wally," I insisted. But, trooper that he was, he just kept coming. I began firing round after round of apples, desperately trying to drive the pigs away from Wally. But it wasn't working.

I leaped to the ground, falling clumsily, yelling at the tree as it grabbed my shoe. Already there was snorting at my heels. Without turning around, I picked Wally up ten yards from the fence, then sprinted as only a scared person could—up and over wood and wire, near a post.

I set Wally down. He started laughing and rolling on the ground. There were few times when my fear and relief were more apparent. My mouth was dry and I was choking. Wally pulled out an apple which he had hung on to during the escape and offered me a bite.

Sitting against the fence I gasped for breath. In my mind I could see little Wally fatally bitten, surrounded by giant pigs.

Wally promised to wait outside the pig orchard while I retrieved my shoe. By the time I had gotten to the tree, Wally was screaming and yelling, attracting half the pigs to the fence with apples thrown from his side.

A sudden weakness from the exertion—maybe it was frustration over Wally—almost overwhelmed me. I exited the pig orchard farther down the reddog road and let Wally run to catch up.

Courtesy of Wally & Bonnie Gerhold
Wally, at 6-years old

Courtesy of Madeline Bowden

NEUTRALIZING CONNIE

Jim emphasized a list of mundane facts: "Cows are dumb animals. They eat grass, drink water occasionally, and give milk in the mornings and evenings. Personality? Nah! Do cows ever think? Never! Do they remember anything? Oh, maybe things like, 'Soo Cow!' the call that brings them to the barn for feeding and milking." I believed all of this--until I experienced Connie's revenge.

Connie provided twice the milk that Merle's other three cows produced, but she was not as congenial. Actually, her behavior was unpredictable. We had to strap her back legs

41

during milking to prevent her from kicking us or doing damage to expensive milk-pumping equipment.

My new job was to secure Connie's back legs, near the knees, by tying a leather strap around them in figure-eight fashion. The first time that I did this, Connie turned her head in the stall, looked back at me, but raised no fuss at all. Then I brought the vacuum milking-assembly into the stall and hooked up Connie. Connie glanced back again, this time with a wild look in her eye. I was glad that she was strapped.

Later that day, I was digging out thistle in the cow pasture; Jim said it was dangerous to grazing animals. Connie saw me and started over. I was dead center in the pasture with no place to escape. The cow stopped and lowered her horns then raised them threateningly, tossing her head back. I decided to leave the pasture at once.

Though keeping her distance, Connie continued to raise and lower her horns as she followed me toward the corner of the pasture. Earlier, Merle had advised me not to run from Connie, but to talk sternly and walk casually away. Finally, I was able to exit the pasture by circling a hay stack near a corner of the electric fence. I mentioned the incident to Jim, who said I had handled the situation well.

For the rest of the week, I got the eye from Connie as I applied the strap. Each day, I practiced buckling it around two small, closely spaced trees to increase my speed.

The following week, Jim and I returned to the pasture to continue digging out thistle. As soon as Jim started back to the barn, Connie saw her chance. She started jumping around like a young colt, running in a large semi-circle around me. I spoke with as deep a voice as a scared fourteen-year-old could muster, "Connie, settle down, girl. Take it easy, Connie." Once again I made it to the haystack and escaped. Jim, watching from the fence, shook his head and said that he'd never seen anything like it. Jim tried to make a feeble joke about the whole thing. I was more shaken than the last time and Jim knew it.

It was hard to accept the fact that this old cow was singling me out for punishment. Maybe she sensed my apprehension and was taking advantage of me.

The climactic event occurred a few days later. Merle had made the comment that some animals were more like horses, others more like mules. "You get tough with a horse, he'll usually take it. But, you punish a mule, and the first chance he gets, he'll kill you. You can't neutralize mules," Merle warned. I thought of Connie with long mule ears.

That evening after supper I was lying in the backyard. Jim was down at the barn bringing in the cows for milking. We planned to go hunting after milking was completed. I had Jim's six-shot rifle and had just pumped several shots into the haystack we used for hanging targets. As I reloaded the clip, Connie stepped from behind the stack. I stood up, dumb with horror, realizing that she could have easily been shot.

The other cows had already found their way to the barn, a full 100 yards away. Connie seemed as shocked as I was. With a sidelong glance, she quickly trotted to the barn to join the other cows.

"I've neutralized that dumb cow," I said to myself.

For the remainder of the summer, Connie appeared to hardly take notice when I strapped her legs or milked her. She usually would raise her head promptly to give me full access to her trough when I brought her a pail of feed. Connie became a more congenial cow. Even so, I didn't go into the pasture when Connie was out of the barn.

BIG BILL

Farm people worked together in what Merle described as a farm cooperative. Mowing and threshing equipment was shared so that each farm didn't have to own every piece of equipment. But, to me, it seemed more than that. It was a working relationship among friends who relied on each other. Everyone seemed to do for everyone else. The closeness of farm people in Washington County was an inspiration to a city boy. Back home in Sheraden, every neighbor's work was different – railroader, steel worker, store owner, barber. This small Pittsburgh neighborhood was a typical Mayberry, USA. But farm life provided a different feeling; one of camaraderie, of happiness and frugal prosperity.

Those on the farm seemed to accept the death of a good milking cow or even a favorite horse as a natural part of life, not a time for great sorrow. But human death was never expected, and never accepted. Especially Bull O'Brian's death.

Big Bill "Bull" O'Brian was as wide as he was tall. And he was strong; a legend throughout the county. Big Bill raised bulls and he sold them for breeding. The bulls respected Big Bill O'Brian because he intimidated them. In the field, his presence was formidable. He didn't take any stuff. O'Brian had no fear. He even walked his bulls to the barn.

We were at Ray's finishing dinner when the phone rang. "My God!" Ray's wife was shaken. "Bill O'Brian's dead!" A bull had moved sideways in a pen and Big Bill was pinned against a wall. His youngest son saw it all happen but had been helpless to act.

JIM

Jim was big at 17, well over six feet, a handsome 200-pounder. He could shoot a rifle like a marksman. He looked forward to evening romps in the woods with Joey, Mitzi's last puppy. Groundhogs and skunks and rabbits and squirrels – he loved them all.

"Always use hollow-point shells. They expand on impact so there's no suffering. And always shoot an extra shot when you kill an animal—for mercy."

Jim went hunting every chance he got.

STARRY COUNTRY NIGHTS

July evenings progressed into August, and warm, breezy evenings. The nights were totally free of city rumblings. The Milky Way was spread across a dark, almost mysterious night sky.

Jim and I had a favorite evening hang-out spot, on the lawn near a large spreading elm, just above the reddog road. We would lie on our backs, with an astronaut's view of every star in the heavens.

I miss starry country nights when the air is clear and the sky is moonless. Hundreds of extra stars, that were hidden by city smoke and rising building heat, winked down through the country night air.

After a late supper, Jim and I were resting in the grass at the side of the farm house on Friday night.

"I think that you like Fran," Jim began.

"Yeah, I do," I said in a matter-of-fact way.

Jim didn't say anything. It was dark, but I could hear his sporadic movements in the grass.

"I do, too," he finally said, "and I wish she'd visit tomorrow when Merle and Stella are at the market." Jim sighed. Fran frequently rode across the farm properties on her horse, Buddy. She was due for a visit soon.

"Yeah, Jim." He sounded like he was in misery. He had these great expectations where Fran was concerned, but when she was around, Jim would become very quiet or else he'd say some nonsense, then laugh like he'd made a great joke.

"There goes a shooting star, Jim!" I gasped, coming to a sitting position. Its bright exodus stunned me, moving instantly from zenith to horizon. The tiny meteor was the brightest light in the heavens for its brief moment of life.

"Yeah," Jim mumbled, feigning interest. "I'll bet Fran likes me, too. I think that she'd admit it if I was alone with her."

"Hey, Jim, do you think the full moon is going to rise tonight? I see some light behind that hill," I queried pleasantly enough.

"Nah, those are farm lights." Jim seemed irritated. There was a moment of silence and then, "Do you think that Fran really likes me—you know, where she and I could get serious, like necking?" Jim's voice sounded a bit higher.

"I don't know, Jim. She's always kidding with you when she stops by on Buddy."

"Hey, if Fran visits tomorrow, you take a hike, okay?" He grabbed at me in the dark. "Is it a deal, buddy?" His comment was half-threat, half-request.

50

"Yeah, Jim, it's a deal." I was rolling over and over down the small hill. Jim couldn't hold on. I was laughing at his clumsiness. He was twice my size, but here he was vulnerable, and wanting my cooperation.

Suddenly there was a comet-like streak to the horizon, then another, then a third. It was an August meteor shower.

"Jim, my God, did you see that!" There was silence. Jim had finally witnessed and felt what I had felt. Here we were, tiny mortals gazing into eternity, seeing stars whose lights were finally reaching us after traveling thousands of years. Many of the stars had probably disappeared and didn't even exist anymore.

I crawled on hands and knees, back up the hill.

"So, what do you think about that, Jim?" I said, still excited about the meteor shower. I heard the slam of the front screen door and realized Jim had gone into the house. When I got there, Stella said he'd gone to bed.

Courtesy of Madeline Bowden

GANDER ATTACK

I smile whenever I hear this line from the musical "Oklahoma":

"Geese and ducks and chicks better scurry,
When I take you out in my surrey, with the fringe on top."

It brings to mind two aggressive farm birds. One bird was a fat, mean spirited gander, the other a skinny, overly aggressive rooster. I think that either one could have made short work of an Oklahoma surrey.

53

Stella still remembers her gander's territorial instincts and aggressiveness, particularly when arthritis returns in her broken right finger.

Back then, Stella's entire duck and gander squad numbered two dozen, maybe a few more. A wandering blanket of white backs and shaking feathered tails waddled across the front yard at will, usually staying within the boundaries of the road, the stream and the barn.

The flock was seldom seen in the field beyond the barn unless it was a brief waddle upstream, then back. Jim received some small delight chasing the ganders around when Merle and Stella were at market.

Geese or ganders, they all looked the same to me. But ganders are territorial, and they could be mean. Much like Whitey, Merle's crazy rooster, you didn't have to provoke Stella's gander for him to attack menacingly. Just approach the yard from the barn or step off the front porch of the house, and the movement could trigger a gander attack. Twenty-five or so pounds, but looking much larger, he would flap and hiss and generally carry on, sometimes rushing directly at you.

Jim knew that I was apprehensive about gander attacks. One day, just as I was stepping onto the porch on my way to the barn, Jim said,

"Stella said to keep a special eye on the gander today. Let me know if he attacks you. He's so sick that Stella thinks he should be given some medicine." Jim patted his pocket. "Only if he attacks, OK?" The screen door slammed loudly as Jim disappeared back into the kitchen.

A dozen ducks and geese were grouped together a few hundred feet off the front porch. I had just started off the porch when a few of the ducks and geese took notice. They started toward me probably hoping for a handout.

Suddenly, Stella's gander turned toward the sound of the screen door, saw some of his flock moving toward me, and attacked. He neck was thrust forward, and his head dancing and weaving, he darted forward with surprising speed. I backed up blindly and jumped the few steps to the relative safety of the porch. "Jim, Stella's gander is at it again."

My yell was drowned by the loud crack of a rifle. The gander's head disappeared, shot completely off.

Jim had cut through the house, out through the side porch, and in one fluid motion had taken aim and fired from the side of the house directly behind me. The gander's long neck and body continued its advance at what appeared to me a quickened pace. A freshly beheaded chicken would do the same thing, running out its life's blood in a final frenzy until it falls dead.

My initial apprehension from the gander's attack, the sound of Jim's rifle discharge and the quickening advance of the headless gander were too much for my brain to process. I ran into the kitchen without bothering to open the screen door. In my desperate attempt to escape the headless thing rushing at me, I had run straight through the screen.

As Jim laughed, I struggled to comprehend what had happened. Jim ducked and stepped through the gaping hole that I had made in the screen.

"The *medicine* in my pocket was this clip full of hollow-point shells," he said, patting the side of his rifle.

"Stella and Merle told me to kill the gander two days ago."
Jim punched me lightly on the shoulder grinning an evil grin.
"I was just waiting for the right moment."

PICKIN' PEACHES

Beyond Merle's house, just before the cucumber patch leading to Ray's pig orchard, there were several rows of peach trees. From the tree I was in, I could watch Connie, the hell-bent Holstein, near the hay stack, chewing her cud and watching out of the side of her eye, hoping I'd join her.

Picking peaches is an art like corn husking. Picking tomatoes or beans has no attraction. It's work..

Peach trees grow close to the ground so there was little danger of injury from a fall. Slippery, oozing tree wax was your only enemy.

Jim was clumsy with size. His long arms could reach farther than mine. If it weren't for the few feet of trunk, he could have cleaned a peach tree standing on the ground.

I'd been climbing trees since I could walk. With my dexterity on all fours, my picking speed was twice Jim's and my pleasure was in his knowing it.

You can't drop this fruit; you lay it gently in your shoulder sack. Peaches had to be emptied often or they'd bruise. Five or six bushels were all we'd pick for market a week. That morning we'd already picked four.

Jim seemed to be more cautious than I, and always kept his eye on the count – his versus mine. I was near the top finishing one tree. I was stretched flat out on the limb and grabbed the last peach that I could reach. A sudden sharp pain numbed my arm from thumb to elbow. It became a stabbing pulse. My thumb felt afire.

I jumped from the tree—maybe fell—bruising some of the peaches. Jim helped me get the stinger out. I described the pain to Jim.

"Yeah, but that sucker will die. He lost his stinger," Jim smiled as he talked—he enjoyed the thought of the bee dying and I had to agree with him.

Jim picked most of the last two bushels. I seemed to hear buzzing noises everywhere. There must have been a hive nearby.

Courtesy of Madeline Bowden

CORNTEST

Jim and I competed. I wasn't near his strength, but I was faster and more agile than he, and desperation made me develop a quick mind to resolve his stunts.

Jim had a ferocious appetite. At one sitting he'd down a quart of milk, two plates of any kind of food, and several slices of homemade bread. This was followed religiously with a fourth of Stella's peach freezer cake.

I was always able to hold my own when it came to eating. Neither Jim nor I needed a rationale for putting away food. One of my favorites was corn-on-the cob. Merle's corn crop was comprised of larger-than-life yellow ears, with perfectly aligned, plump, almost sweet kernels.

On one thing Jim and I agreed: The corn ears were the biggest and tastiest we had ever eaten. Fresh from the pot, coated with farm butter and a touch of salt, corn-on-the-cob was a real feast.

"I could probably eat you under the table," Jim commented one day.

You had to respect Jim's pride in his consumptive skills. But he did not have the taste for corn that I had.

"Jim, I'll think about taking that bet, if you let me pick the kind of food, and the time."

"As long as it isn't dog food," he said.

"It's corn-on-the-cob, tomorrow, at lunch."

I felt reassured by my own voice. Jim gave me his finest country-boy smile. Stella laughed. It was definitely on.

The next morning at breakfast, Jim, as usual, ate a goodly portion of everything in sight. Perhaps he had forgotten my challenge. I limited myself to milk, corn flakes, and juice.

As Jim rose from the table to follow Merle and me to the barn, he turned to Stella.

"Don't forget the 'Corntest' at lunch." She nodded, laughing. I said nothing.

By noon, the day had heated up. The cool of the porch was welcome as we walked single file into the kitchen and sat down. Stella had picked and cooked some of the largest ears of corn she could find. It was going to be a great contest.

Jim seemed to rake the entire first cob clean with one motion.

"There's no hurry, Jim," I suggested.

"Hungry," he said, quickly cleaning a second cob.

I consoled myself with the thought that his teeth were bigger than mine. In fact, his whole mouth was bigger than mine. I methodically crunched yellow row after yellow row.

When four huge, well-cleaned cobs lay on Jim's plate, he began to slow noticeably. I had finished two ears and had two on standby.

Well into his fifth ear, Jim glanced over with a big grin. "Man, is this stuff good!"

I agreed, smiling back and eyeing No. 4.

Finally, I was through my fifth ear, sucking loudly on the bottom end, and licking my lips. As I started to feel full, I decided to use some psychology. We were dead even on six.

"I'll rest my teeth a minute," Jim said, smiling faintly.

I concluded that his stomach pain matched mine. Finished with ear No. 6, I forced myself to start nonchalantly buttering ear No. 7.

Jim seemed deeply engrossed in thought. He stared at his uneaten seventh cob and slowly rotated it in his hand. I started my routine—two rows top-to-bottom, then, two rows bottom-to-top. The corn had become tasteless. My stomach ached. Jim watched me finish No. 7.

"Well, I can't eat another kernel," he admitted finally. "You win." Jim had not touched his seventh ear. Rising slowly from the table, he eased his belt out one notch.

It was a glorious victory. Merle and Stella both said they were impressed. I wouldn't be able to stomach corn for years, thanks to the Corntest. But I had beaten Jim.

Barely able to move, I turned to look at Jim's face. He was in the alcove across the kitchen, near the refrigerator. He had cut himself a fourth of Stella's peach freezer cake and was wolfing it down.

HEREFORD TO "HEIFER"

Storms came on quickly in the late spring. This one had started during the night, but continued unabated into the work day. I came out on the porch to watch the rain descend in sheets, and march wave after wave across the yard and against the barn. It was the kind of rain that usually stops after a brief heavy downpour, but this one lingered on.

"We'll be working in Ray's barn today," Merle said, passing me on the porch and beckoning me to the car. Merle spun the vehicle around in the mud and gravel driveway, and careened the half mile to his brother Ray's farm. Merle was cussing the bad roads and praising the great Buicks, and intermittently humming to himself. He was pleasant enough.

Because of the continuing storm, it had started to thunder, Merle and Ray worked in Ray's barn. They had managed to isolate a young Hereford bull calf in a side room where Ray normally kept a new tractor. But the tractor was outside under a protruding roof. Merle had cut off the only exit to the room. It was just Merle, Ray, me and the few-week-old Hereford.

"We're making a Hereford into a heifer," Merle stated casually, watching my curiosity.

"What's the difference, Merle? Isn't a heifer a young cow?"

Merle was waiting for my question.

"Ray, he wants to know 'what's the difference.'" Ray was busy fitting a small rubber band over a special pair of pliers and trying not to laugh at Merle's game. "Merle, tell that young farmer to bulldog that baby bull. We've got work to do."

I quickly set out after the young bull. It would run and turn and dart, sometimes toward me, until I didn't know who was intimidated more. The small bull's aggressiveness was obvious.

Merle and Ray let me suffer a while longer, then Ray handed me the pliers while he and Merle got the bull stopped and tied. It wasn't easy for them and that made me feel a lot better.

Once the bull was down, they quickly positioned the rubber band around its testicles and released it.

"What will that do?" I asked.

"Hell, it'll castrate him. No circulation for a month and his testicles will fall off. Then he'll become a steer, not a heifer." Merle smiled, "I was kidding about the bull becoming a heifer" Merle continued in his matter-of fact way. "Then he'll get heavier, and grow bigger for meat. Now, you always wanted to be bigger, c'mon, we'll do it to you next." Merle grabbed me.

Ray yelled, "I've got this gadget ready to go again. Hold him, Merle." Ray grabbed my arm. Merle had me by the back of the belt. My adrenaline was still pumping from the bulldogging. Wresting the pliers from Ray's hand, I threw them outside the barn where they quickly sank into the mud. Merle was laughing so hard, he could barely shove me out the door. "You find them or we will castrate you," he gasped.

Ray was bent over, his hands on his knees, laughing and shaking his head.

They didn't let me back into the barn.

NIGHT VISION

$\mathbf{F}$requently, after the evening milking, Jim and I would go hunting. Jim had a semi-automatic, 6-shot, Winchester 22 rifle with a six-power scope. Mine was a single shot, J.C. Higgins.

We'd hunt for groundhogs and skunks. If an occasional rabbit or squirrel showed itself, we considered that fair game, too. Birds, mice, hawks, large bees, you name it—they were all potential victims.

Groundhogs were easy if you caught them either in the open or poking their heads up from their nest holes in the ground. We knew where most of the holes were around the farm. With Jim's six-power rifle scope, he used the fields like a shooting gallery. Up would come the cautious head of the groundhog; off went the shot, off went the head. However, squirrels and rabbits were more cautious and evasive. We shot few of these.

Skunks were also easy once you found their hideouts, usually under corn cribs, around other out-buildings, or in rock piles. Once discovered, they usually ignored you and slowly walked away with a cautious tail spray-cocked upright to baptize the air skunk-style. The smell was a humbling experience. To return to the farm carrying their lingering odor was taboo.

Merle's young pup Joey followed us on one particular hunt. Nothing showed because of Joey's yipping. It was almost dark, but Jim said it didn't matter. He said he had night vision. We were in a field across the road from Ray's driveway when Joey found two skunks near a wood pile.

With a couple of shots, Jim made quick work of the larger, lumbering male.

"One for mercy," he explained. I thought that he had missed with the first shot.

The second skunk was headed toward the nearby creek just below the road. Joey was anxiously in pursuit. My shells were all spent from target practicing on tree limbs earlier.

From the brush near the stream, Joey was whining and yipping, rubbing his eyes with his paws.

"Skunk spray has blinded many a dog," Jim yelled angrily.

Meanwhile, the skunk wandered back in front of us, his tail up and walking a little funny. Jim aimed at the skunk and emptied his clip at point-blank range. The skunk continued his slow exodus and disappeared into rocks and grass close to the wood pile.

"Boy, that's some skunk! I'll run over to Ray's and get more shells," I suggested.

"Don't bother," Jim yelled. "I couldn't have missed at this range. He's gone off somewhere to die."

I was closest to Joey. The pup was in misery and kept running away. Finally, holding him down, I was able to wash off his eyes and head. Jim was standing with his back to the wood pile, watching us and glancing occasionally toward the rocks where the skunk had disappeared. The skunk spray from Joey was already part of me. I prayed that I'd receive some sort of second wind. Like a runner nearing exhaustion, my brain was reeling from insufficient oxygen.

Suddenly, Jim took off his shirt, holding it open, blocking my view of the rocks and wood pile.

"Here, wrap Joey in this," he said nervously, glancing back once again toward the rocks.

"We'll both be sleeping in the barn tonight, Jim."

"Yeah, let's get him home." Jim took Joey in his arms and quickly walked up the rise to the road in the near-dark.

I glanced back toward the rocks and grass near the woodpile. In the semi-darkness, I spotted the small skunk, tail still raised, momentarily waddling into view, and disappearing into its wood pile home. Jim's night vision had failed. At point-blank range, he had missed the skunk with four shots.

Jim was already up to the road, fifty yards ahead and walking fast. In spite of the "skunk smoke," I was laughing pretty hard. I waited awhile before I told him what he already knew.

HUSKIN' CORN

I recall my first experience picking corn. It was a cool, overcast August day. Jim approached with two large canvas bags. He tossed one toward me explaining that it took plenty of effort, plain and simple, to master the art of corn huskin'. And it took practice to select only the plumpest, worm-free ears of corn from acres of seven-foot-high stalks. Jim and I collected the corn in canvas bags that easily held several dozen large ears.

With his fingers, a corn husker feels each mature ear to test for plumpness. Once he has found a large, solid ear, he peels the top leaves and corn silk back a few inches to check for worms. Only worm-free ears are selected for market. The rest are fed to the chickens.

Jim and I began husking corn in the middle of the cornfield. We worked, one to the right, the other to the left, down the long rows. Jim explained that this was a natural approach for us.

"I'm left-handed, so I'll cover the rows to the left. That way the corn I pick will be closest to my best hand. You're right-handed, so you cover the rows to the right. We're a natural team. If we switched places, we'd be turning and twisting our backs to reach for each ear of corn, and fighting the bag. It wouldn't be natural."

This all sounded reasonable enough. Jim had a year's husking experience on me. He was fast. I could cover a row in fifteen minutes or less. Frequently, Jim would finish a row and be well into the next row and I'd still be struggling many yards down his finished row. Jim's knowledge gave him a feeling of power. He wanted to be in control of the whole job. At first, I accepted this because Jim provided a helping hand occasionally. I was always behind and he seemed anxious to help.

"Whoops, I found another wormy one in your batch," he'd say. "Here, let's throw this sucker away." To make the point, he'd wind up and pitch like Merle doing one of his minor-league deliveries, then throw the ear far out into the field.

After several sessions of husking, I discovered a few things about Jim's "helping hand." If he found a mature ear of corn, he wouldn't always check for worms before removing it and placing it in his bag. This kept him ahead of me in picking speed. Yet, if he found worms in one that he had already picked for me, I was blamed.

Finally I pointed this out to Jim in my tactless way. I was ignored. But his speed suddenly slowed. I found myself matching him ear for ear—and he didn't discover any more wormy ears in my husking bag. After exposing Jim's game, I lost his help toward the end of that day.

I was mystified by Jim's husking speed when he worked on his own, but I had my suspicions. One afternoon, Merle came out to the field earlier than usual with the tractor and a wagon to help pick up the many baskets of husked corn.

While I was explaining to Merle Jim's left-hander, right-hander husking theory, Jim interrupted.

"Merle knows all that. He even knows that I've been left-handed all my life." Jim seemed nervous and uneasy.

"Yeah, Jim, but does Merle know how fast you are," I queried, "and how fast you picked the lower section?"

Merle started laughing. "Jim, do you always take this lower section like I used to? Hell, I thought I told you to switch every once in a while?"

Jim began explaining his left-hander, right-hander theory in great detail. Merle was laughing harder, agreeing with Jim and winking at me.

"Did you tell our young friend here, Jim, that the lower section has shorter rows? It's damn near five-six yards shorter at the lower end where we didn't plant."

Jim stood scratching an arm, mumbling that he thought I needed the practice. Merle was chuckling to himself and slapped me on the shoulder.

"I guess I need practice too, Jim." With some fanfare, Merle grabbed a basket of corn with his left hand and started to clumsily pull it across the ground toward the wagon. He motioned to me for help. "Help me with your right hand here. Without Jim's left hand to get these up on the wagon, we'll probably be out here 'til midnight."

MOUSE POWER

Harvesting wheat and oats dominated the late summer days. Each summer, the farmers joined together to help each other thresh and bale hay and straw, and bag wheat and oat seed on the local farms.

Jim and I were usually relegated to collecting seed in burlap bags. The seed belched in a thick stream from the side of a stationary thresher.

I can remember winning Jim's respect that day. What he didn't know was that it was all the fault of a field mouse.

Jim was a competitor at seventeen. He earned the name "Big Jim" during that summer, growing well over six feet and an even 200 pounds. I was fourteen, and by the end of summer, husky at five-eight and 140 pounds.

We were working Ray's farm. The stationary thresher was consuming loose shocks of hay at a rapid pace and producing baled hay from one end. Jim and I would grab the bales with hooks and throw them up on a hay wagon. From the thresher's middle belched a stream of wheat grain which fell into one of two wooden boxes positioned on the ground. Two boxes of grain filled a burlap sack. Grabbing a neatly folded piece of burlap from a large pile, I would go down on one knee, pulling open the sack with both hands and swooping my right elbow down into the sack to create an opening into which Jim would pour the dusty grain.

So it went through the morning hours: a bale of hay onto the wagon, two boxes of grain into the burlap. Occasionally, Jim would pour the grain from a standing position so that I would receive the full effect of dust coming off the grain. If I wasn't alert to Jim's game, I breathed the grain dust, choking or sneezing. Jim took great delight in catching me off guard.

I'd lift a bale of hay up and onto the wagon. Because of my size, I was forced to give it a shove with my chest to position it on the edge of the wagon, and give it a simultaneous push with my arms to deliver it to the waiting farm hand atop the wagon. Jim, with his extra height and reach, performed the same job in one smooth motion. Occasionally, he'd give me a big grin to make sure that I was aware of his strength and ability.

During one of my carries to the hay wagon, I noticed a squirming field mouse caught in the dirt under the wagon handle. I carefully lifted the heavy wooden tongue with both hands and moved it slightly off the flattened mouse. It lay still, probably getting its breath. Unwisely, I picked the mouse up by the tail. It quickly swung up, biting my finger to the bone.

"You damn sucker!" I shouted, throwing him as hard as I could, into the field.

Jim turned and saw the anger and misery on my face. He hadn't observed the mouse incident and he took the assault personally. I was fed up with him so I kept glaring. He shook his head, then quietly grabbed a burlap sack from the pile, lowered himself to one knee, and swooped his elbow down into the sack to make the opening.

Now that's mouse power, I thought, watching Jim suppress a sneeze as I poured the box of grain from above. I found pouring grain into burlap sacks an exhilarating experience for the rest of that quiet afternoon.

ELECTRIC FENCES

On Saturdays, when Merle and Stella drove into the Southside Pittsburgh Farmers' Market to sell chickens, corn-on-the cob and other vegetables, eggs and butter, farm work kept Jim and me plenty busy. But on Saturday evenings, in the hours before Merle and Stella returned, we sometimes went a little crazy, like the time we played with the electric fence.

Electric fences are necessary to contain large farm animals. Coming in contact with the barbed wire causes an immediate jolt. It's not heart stopping, but an animal, once shocked, probably doesn't want to experience the effect more than is necessary. What this boils down to is that the grass on the other side of the fence just may not be worth the pain.

Jim would play a leaf game at the fence near the barn, touching various sizes and different kinds of leaves to the fence. Some leaves triggered immediate pain—a paralyzing streak up the arm. Leaf size didn't seem to matter. Some would give a small tingle, others a large jolt. I laughed at Jim's preoccupation with pain.

One Saturday, to demonstrate his abilities, Jim dared me to play a game at the electric fence gate next to the barn. He explained that we would each take the same kind of leaf and see who could hold a leaf to the electric fence the longest. He assured me that electric current passing through this particular leaf blunted the full shock to an irritating buzz. However, I was to find out that a single second was a long time. I recalled, years earlier, accidentally shocking myself more than once testing a wall plug. The jolts seemed worse as I grew up. I accepted Jim's dare, figuring that with his size he was a walking time-bomb.

It turned in my favor. No matter how hard Jim tried, he couldn't hold out as long as I. Through the leaf the buzz paralyzed my arm from finger to elbow. When I finally let go, the fingers were cramped and cold, even though the effort had taken no more than several seconds. Jim looked frustrated but said nothing.

Later, when I fed the calf her milk at the barn gate, as always, I turned off the electric fence for a few minutes. Calf was on one side of the fence; I was on the other. I didn't think Jim was aware that I took this precaution.

I remember that it was Jim's last weekend at Merle and Stella's before he had to depart and help his family move to a farm in the next county. It was Saturday, and Merle and Stella had spent the day at the farmers' market.

Jim and I had finished the evening milking. We followed our usual routine. Jim went up to the chicken houses to feed the chickens and gather eggs. I filtered the milk, saved two quarts for house use, and put the rest through a cream separator. Cream was collected in the cold storage room and churned to butter biweekly. Excess skim milk was fed to the pigs, the cats, and Calf, Merle's only calf.

I had just carried the excess skim milk down to the barn in two buckets. In one, I mixed pig feed and dandelion leaves. This concoction was poured into the pig trough. The six pigs, grunting and squealing as they vied for position, waded into the trough. It wasn't ice cream but they loved the stuff.

For Calf's feeding, I mixed a large scoop of cow feed in with her milk. The feed bins were at the back of the barn near the electric fence switch. I switched off the electricity and walked out to Calf, who waiting expectantly on the other side of the fence. Calf was almost belligerent in her approach to eating. In a few brief minutes, she had finished off her meal and stepped back.

Jim quietly approached me from behind. He grabbed me in a bear hug, and with his superior size, pushed me over the electric gate wire.

"With these gloves on, I'm not feeling anything." He almost growled the words. The fence was turned off but I carried on like it was killing me.

"I'm telling Merle," I threatened, "and your older brother. Let me go!"

Jim's older brother, George, a veteran with the Purple Heart and a medal for valor, would frequently force Jim to scratch his back. George had this thing about having his back scratched. Once he had shot Jim with a B-B gun for not scratching his back on command. Jim respected George and reluctantly catered to his requests. On the other hand, George always treated me fine.

"My family will be long gone to our farm at Raccoon State Park when you get back home, you clown—so fry." Jim laughed like he was insane, and followed up with more pressure against the wire.

I was completely helpless, bent over the wire until I could see only the dirt on my shoes. I was in no real pain. But the wire gate held firm.

Suddenly, Jim released his hold on me and disappeared into the barn mumbling like a mad man. I figured that my threats and suffering had intimidated him. Quickly regaining my composure, I walked into the barn to turn on the electric fence. Jim blocked my way.

"I turned it on before I fried you," he yelled.

"Are you sure, Jim?" I countered. "Merle wants that electricity on." I backed out the door deciding that in Jim's crazed state, discretion was in order.

Studying the situation, I slowly walked over to the electric gate. Why hadn't it shocked me? I decided that I would give it a quick swipe with my bare hand. I did. The jolt stiffened my entire body for an instant. I was startled by the power of the shock and fell backward, sitting down hard.

Then I saw Jim. He was on the pasture side of the barn hanging onto the large exit door. He had swung out and around to face me. "Gotcha, sucker," he yelled, grinning broadly, then disappeared as the door swung back toward the barn.

'MATOR WAR

On the farm story-telling was an art. It was a way of relating recent news, or old news, or oft-told local epics – hand-me-down stories of courage, strength and will.

Merle seemed to know them all, and could shape and relate an interesting story with the best of them. His fellow farmers savored his unique humor, his bluntness, his added new twists and turns to old stories.

Jim and I found it hard to compete with Merle's story-telling. But I'm fairly sure we left Merle with at least one good yarn.

While we were eating lunch one day, Jim and I described a game we played occasionally at a movie theater. During the matinee, usually at the height of the action – or during a love scene – I'd jump up holding the back of my neck.

"Who flung that 'mator?" I'd yell. Jim would be sitting in the balcony, and slowly stand to his full 6 feet 3 inches.

"I flung that 'mator!" he'd respond. I'd slowly sit down rubbing my neck. "Boy, you can sure flung 'er."

Merle chuckled about the story during the remainder of lunch.

Now, tomatoes were a popular market item at the farm. A good market tomato was bright red, meaty, but firm to the touch. Weekly, Jim and I were down on our haunches for hours, duck-walking through dusty, hay strewn rows of tomato vines.

During late summer's picking time, the many rows of tomato plants became a field of foot deep snarls. After a few hours in the fields, we did anything for a diversion.

One particularly hot mid-morning, I took a moment to rest and eat one of Merle's tomatoes.

I heard a dull thud next to my boot. Jim had thrown a soft tomato from about 10 yards away.

"Wake up and start picking, "Jim yelled. Then he turned and stooped over his work, leaving as a target a back as broad as a cow's belly from my uphill position.

He didn't suspect I would retaliate. Jim couldn't imagine any 13 year-old kid being an aggressor against a 200-pound 17 year-old.

But I had learned long ago how to properly fling tomatoes. If you threw them like a baseball, the force of the throw ruptures the tomato, splattering over your hand and sending only the core toward your target. No, you had to throw a rotten tomato with the palm of the hand, pushing it forward like a shot putter.

I continued picking tomatoes, working my position closer to Jim's back. I deposited large, soft tomatoes (additional ammo) along my escape route toward the chicken yard and the house.

The sudden thud covered my boot and lower pant leg with tomato seeds and pulp. Jim's smile of satisfaction over a second direct hit was followed by some more mother-henning. Then he went back to work.

The arc was perfect. For a moment, I lost it in the sun as the two-pound projectile gained altitude. Then gravity took over and it made impact—a sound like a rock hitting deep mud. Tomato pulp exploded across Jim's back, neck and arms, and began to slide down the back of his dungarees as he fell forward.

He never recovered from the shock. I gave four or five additional volleys, some of which found his boots and legs. By then, I was out of Jim's range and headed for the chicken yard.

Jim finally showed up at the house. He had tried to wash off at the stream, but his T-shirt remained pink and spotted with seeds.

Jim finally appeared at the lunch table with fresh T-shirt, pants, and carrying his socks.

Soon Merle arrived, viewing with some amusement Jim's pink T-shirt hanging over the porch railing.

"Who flung that 'mator?" he said, suppressing a laugh. I slowly stood up. "I flung that 'mator!"

Jim was looking at his plate. Finally, he returned my look and broke into a grin. "You can sure flung 'er."

AUGUST SHOWER

The sky was deep, dark and clear.
Stars sparkled like moonlit rain frozen;
When, far in the north sky—it seemed so near--
A bright meteor speared the horizon.

My ears seemed ready for a resonance,
Like thunder rolls after a lightning strike.
I sat immobile, not daring to chance
Missing a second streak across the night.

Marveling at the speed of its decent,
I wondered, was it really there at all?
Was this an isolated incident,
Or were others also about to fall?

Standing slowly, I gained a wider view.
The stars seemed to breath in their velvet night;
When, suddenly, the event began anew,
As many meteors took their southern flight.

The silent drama diminished me.
I, a mortal, with mortal fantasy,
Mere dust on an orb of sky and sea;
This orb mere dust of a galaxy.

Courtesy of Madeline Bowden

CHAWIN' HABIT

It was a few days after the great tomato war that Jim and I and a large group of farmers from neighboring farms were gathered to help with threshing wheat on a section of Ray's, Merle's brother's farm.

Mowing machines cut the wheat grass, then straightened and tied the straw into armful-size bundles. The bunches or "shocks" as we called them, were immediately collected by hand. Five were placed on end in a circle with a sixth spread over the top as a moisture barrier.

89

Shocking wheat is man's work. It's a ritual, starting at sunup, stopping for lunch in the grand style of farm lunches and continuing until sunset.

The crew, comprised of local farmers from a farm co-op (everybody pitched in to help each farmer mow and thresh their farm) was grateful for all the help. And everybody was in fine spirits.

While we worked, the farmers' wives were busy at the house preparing a grand luncheon feast. But I wouldn't be eating lunch that day. I was destined to learn a valuable lesson.

One of the crew was a farmer who looked Chinese. I watched as he chewed tobacco then spit it out. I wondered why he had to get rid of it so often. Finally, I asked him.

"Well, it tastes like chocolate after you chew it awhile," he said pensively. "You spit very far and hit anything you aim at." I'm sure he watched my eyes light up as he pinged a few rails.

I memorized the easy way his fingers grasped and measured the chaw. I wanted to know all the moves.

I took a fresh wad. He showed me how to hold it in my cheek, up high. I didn't like the sharp tobacco taste, but the thought of long spits and deadly accuracy drove me on.

We kept moving and shocking. It was hot. Everyone was shirtless as we worked across the field. The tobacco became separated and moist in my mouth. Its juice thinned the saliva. I could spit long trails.

But this wasn't my game. The stuff stung my tongue. Forgetting, I swallowed it. My stomach burned with nausea.

The farmer knew I was sick. He saw me stagger.

90

"Are you dizzy?" he asked.

"Yes," I answered, meekly. "I swallowed the wad, and I'm as sick as a dog."

"You spit with it, you don't eat it," he explained. He looked pensive again. "Do you want some more?" he asked.

"No," I said, becoming sicker at the thought of it.

My habit was cured before it ever started.

Courtesy of Madeline Bowden

WHITEY'S END

There are things that are outside our understanding. The peculiar antics of a few farm animals were a particular wonder to me.

I continued to learn farm work from my friend, Jim, who had worked on Merle's farm the previous summer. One of the chores was chicken-coop cleaning.

With a couple of hundred grown chickens in each of two 20-by-50 foot attached coops, the coops needed cleaning weekly. Eggs were collected morning and evening.

Chicken food consisted of corn, chicken feed, scratch (bits of seeds and other roughage), water, and vegetable scraps. Food and water levels were checked morning and evening. Each Friday, seven chickens were killed and cleaned for Saturday sale at the Southside Pittsburgh Farmers' Market. Merle used a miniature guillotine to decapitate the chickens, which were usually young, full-grown roosters.

Eggs were also taken to market weekly; but first, the eggs had to be washed and inspected for "rooster work," Merle's name for it. We would pass each egg over a special lighted container to check for blood specks in the egg white.

Chicken farming was not exciting. You fed them, collected their eggs, cleaned their coops, and, of course, defeathered and cleaned the unlucky seven for market each week.

We had a name for one of the roosters—Whitey. He was a special bird, and singled me out the first time I visited the chicken yard. Unprovoked, Whitey flew across the yard. He screamed a deep, guttural squawk and ran up against the chicken-wire fence, flapping menacingly. Jim knew all about Whitey and blamed him for most of the specks found in the hens' eggs.

That rooster weighed no more than a few skinny pounds. The other full-grown roosters were bigger and heavier. For this reason, Whitey had little to fear from the guillotine. The most impressive thing about the rooster was the size of his comb. It was bright, blood red and drooped ponderously over to one side.

When Whitey strutted his stuff, he looked larger. The bird had a lot of mature feathers on his tail and wings, and used these to full advantage. Screaming his unique, deep rooster crow, Whitey's head would bolt forward, his wings would spread and flap, and he would dance, on tip-toe, at high speed across the yard. Merle said that Whitey was the first insane chicken that he'd owned.

"Sooner or later, I'll have to kill that one," he said shaking his head in disgust. "He hurts himself more than anything else. Just damn mean."

A few days after Whitey's initial threat, the rooster was in the chicken yard, about 30 yards from where I was walking by, when he began one of his screaming charges. Selecting a smooth, oval-shaped stone, I did an underarm fling directly at the charging bird. An unbelievable shot, the rock hit Whitey square in the gullet, causing his neck and head to jerk back like he was in seizure.

Momentarily the rooster seemed to lose his orientation. He strutted in a semi-circle and charged again, his mouth wide open. But no sound came from his throat. He halted his charge and resumed strutting in a circular fashion. I figured that he was clearing his throat. He suddenly charged again, his mouth fully open, his comb redder than fire. But there was no sound. Finally, confused and unable to fathom what had happened, Whitey retreated into the coop.

From that day on, the crazy rooster's attitude changed. Merle said that Whitey must have "got religion," and chuckled as the bird began to gain weight. A few days after the incident, the rooster developed a high-pitched squeak for a voice. By the fall of that year, Whitey blended so well with the other roosters that we could only identify him by his new voice.

One week, after seven more chickens were guillotined, cleaned and taken to market, we didn't hear Whitey's high-pitched squeak anymore.

SPAGHETTI AND CHICKS

Merle, Jim and I were helping complete the morning threshing at a neighbor's farm. The farm owners, an Italian family, were part of Merle and Ray's farm cooperative. Large farming equipment and chores were shared among several farms reducing farming expenses and shortening the time to harvest. That day farm wives had spent the morning at the farmhouse preparing a lunch feast for the workers.

Most of the crew had left the fields and entered the house. Jim, always hungry, arrived a few minutes later. The Italian farmer's two teenage sons motioned for Jim to sit next to them and enjoy homemade, freshly cooked Italian spaghetti and warm baked bread. They obviously knew Jim's appetite, because one or the other of them kept Jim's plate filled with spaghetti. Jim accepted his good fortune and immediately, without formality, downed two full plates of spaghetti. It was hard to keep track of Jim's voracious eating, and the two farm boys keeping his plate overflowing.

I noticed smiles on the other farmers' faces as they watched Jim consume his lunch. Jim loosened his belt a notch. We all turned to see what the commotion was in the kitchen. Several women emerged carrying steaming plates and bowls of food. In addition to spaghetti, there was corn-on-the-cob, beef stew, several kinds of greens, and gravy, and potatoes, and much more. Jim had finished off his second or third piece of buttered bread and did an immediate double-take when he realized he had filled up on the first course of the meal. We were laughing at Jim's folly. Merle was congratulating the two sons for pulling off a good one on Jim. The Italian farmer's wife, suddenly aware of Jim's eating dilemma, apologized for serving the meal late, but was trying not to laugh.

The lunch crowd of a dozen or more workers became quiet as everyone passed around the platters and bowls and pitched in to eat. It was shortly afterwards that I wandered out onto the front porch looking to rib Jim a bit, but really trying to feel better about gorging myself with too much good food.

Merle was watching the farmer's three-year-old daughter. She was sitting near an overgrown Rhode Island Red rooster, under a large shade tree. Merle explained that the little girl and the chicken were friends – sort of.

I didn't understand his comment until the little girl raised her hand to pet the chicken. The rooster quickly pecked at one of the little girl's fingers and ran off. The little girl yelled, held her finger, complaining to herself, then preached some choice gibberish to the retreating rooster, waving her hand up and down in a threatening gesture, and looking very sad.

The chicken appeared oblivious to it all, nonchalantly pecking at something on the ground. Every time the little girl would attempt to approach and discipline the rooster, the large bird would run a distance, and continue its nonchalant pecking.

Merle and I lost interest and got into a long discussion about something. We were joined by Jim, and were about to go back to the fields when Merle tapped me on the shoulder, pointing toward the shade tree. There was the Rhode Island Red, hunkered down in the dust. The little girl had dozed off, her arm resting across the big rooster's back.

JIM'S DEPARTURE

It was following the threshing season when Jim left Merle and Stella's employ to join his family on their new farm, an hour's drive west of Washington County. There was the usual hand-shaking and wishing of good luck. Jim hugged Stella. She poked him hard in the ribs and winked at me. "Don't boss anyone around on your new farm, Jim." Stella obviously knew Jim's penchant for wanting to lord over everyone. We were all laughing as Merle, Jim, and I got into the car for the drive to the McMurray bus stop.

Jim asked Merle his opinion about raising strawberries and selling them in bulk. Merle agreed that it was a good idea. We fell silent as we passed the end of Dutch's property.

I announced to Jim and Merle the shortcut Jim had taken the first day I arrived.

"There's Dutch's hill, Jim."

Jim scratched his neck, but said nothing. Merle was chuckling to himself and started singing.

"It's fair weather, when good friends get together." Jim gave Merle a serious look and we all laughed. Merle told one joke after another for the rest of the too-short trip. It was a glorious departure.

QUEENIE'S REVENGE

I remained at Merle and Stella's farm hoping to prove myself. My idea was to be invited back to work on the farm on weekends, after school began. Merle seemed to accept me as Jim's successor. Stella appeared happy enough with the arrangement, and even discussed it by phone with my parents.

It was about a week after Jim's departure. I had been sizing up a situation at a recently built home up the road. Later, I would look back on the incident and blame myself for an outcome that was almost predictable.

Queenie was large, and snowy white. Someone said she was a Siberian Spitz. Her temperament was vicious. I had no use for the dog. Her owners had just completed building their home, across Old Venetia Road at the far corner of Merle's property.

Queenie had a "liberty leash." That's what Merle called it. The chain was at least 30 feet long, allowing the dog to travel the length of the gravel driveway during her frenzied barking attacks.

To miss Queenie's act, it was necessary to sneak up the other side of the road through Merle's cucumber field, and cut through the pig orchard. Ray's pigs had the option of either treeing you or driving you back onto the road toward Queenie on her liberty leash. Fortunately, the pigs usually hung out at the other end of the orchard.

When the new neighbors weren't home, Queenie received my taunts. My comment to Merle was that Queenie was all fluff and bluff. Merle laughed heartily.

One afternoon the new neighbors were out in their back yard. Merle and I were walking home to lunch, down the road from the cucumber patch where we had been harrowing a new plot. Merle decided to stop and introduce himself. A four- or five-year-old girl, in a white jumper dress, was between us and Queenie's frenzied approach. The chain leash was singing through the driveway gravel as the dog came bounding up. The hair on the back of my neck rose. My only thought was to get the little girl away from the dog.

Instinctively, I reached out to use a football maneuver and stiff-arm Queenie with my left arm while picking up the girl with my right. The dog's teeth raked the joints of my middle fingers, and cracked the nails. As I spun away, Queenie bit through my dungarees and into my back knee near the tendon.

The little girl was shaken and screaming. The girl's mother was running toward me, reaching for the crying girl. The owner was yelling at the dog. Merle was yelling at the owner to pull the dog away. Queenie was choking at the end of the liberty leash. I was down on my knees, bleeding and spent.

The new neighbor immediately drove me to a doctor in Finleyville. The doctor brush-scrubbed the wounds with soap and covered them.

"The dog will die first if it's rabid, then you'll need shots," he said, patting me sympathetically on the shoulder. Queenie had gotten her revenge, I thought. Now, out of plain spite, she'll probably die, and I'll need those shots.

It was a quiet ride back to the farm. The new neighbor apologized for Queenie's behavior. He explained that the dog belonged to the little girl—his daughter.

Merle lost my help for three days while I mended.

Queenie lived.

105

CAT N' CALF

Summer days turned into fall days. The mornings seemed cooler, the nights damper, the grass was covered with dew. After the threshing season, farm chores became routine. Hoeing what was left of the small bean patch, or cultivating a few dozen rows of the remaining cucumbers was the excitement of the day.

Merle and I had returned from an afternoon of plowing and harrowing in a small field where the previous year he had grown tomatoes and corn. As we approached the barn, we were met by an entourage of half-grown kittens.

In addition to the fully grown cats, there were seventeen kittens at the farm. Merle had explained that cats were important to farmers. They killed rats and mice and other small vermin. Sixteen of Merle's kittens were nameless, but one small tiger-striped kitten had an unusual personality. We called her "Cat" so that we could talk about some of her antics. Cat was a natural mimic. She would observe two or more of the other kittens sparring. To imitate them, she'd spar with herself. During any tussle, you would see Cat involved in her private little war on the sidelines of the real action.

Cat had another idiosyncrasy. She had an affinity for Merle's small calf. Calf didn't seem to mind Cat's hanging around; in fact, they had been together since Cat was born a few months earlier near Calf's stall. I worried that sooner or later Calf wouldn't see Cat and would trample her.

"Hey, there's Cat n' Calf together down by the gate," Jim or I would yell. "You can tell it's milking time." During evening milking, the kittens would hang around the barn near their milk bowls. Cat would wait near the pasture gate.

Each evening, following milking, we strained whole milk for family use. Then, using an electric separator, we collected cream to churn for butter. We fed skim milk to the kittens, Calf, and the pigs.

One evening while walking toward the barn with a bucket of skim milk, I noticed Cat, off by herself, pursuing an invisible enemy, pantomiming the leap and kill tactics of the larger cats. Cat could do a backward somersault, so there she was, jumping an invisible enemy who had foolishly approached from behind.

She seemed to derive great satisfaction from these experiences. Earlier in the summer, Jim had explained that Cat probably had poor eyesight or was completely blind in one eye, which would cause her to have a loss of depth perception. Fighting on the sidelines of a cat foray, Cat might have thought that she was actually in the middle of the fight in her limited, two-dimensional world.

I began to pour the skim milk into the kittens' dishes. As usual, the hungrier kittens wallowed quickly into the bowls to stand knee-deep and lap milk around them. I continued to pour, matting their heads and drowning their ears. They didn't seem to mind.

True to Cat's style, she ignored the kittens' free-style milk medley and followed me over to Calf. Calf was anxiously awaiting supper near the pasture gate. There was nothing lady-like about Calf's approach to drinking milk. She would plunge her face into the liquid, immersing her nostrils at times, and make quick work of a gallon or more of milk, all the while acting oblivious to the world around her. I held the bucket between my boots to keep her from turning it over.

Cat watched Calf down the milk. Then, during one of Calf's swallows when her head must have been raised just enough to leave an opening, Cat leaped up on the buckets' rim and slid like a snake into the remaining half-gallon of milk. Calf ignored Cat and continued her voracious gulping. I spotted Cat lapping milk against the side of the bucket near Calf's submerged chin. Calf quickly finished off the remaining milk, gave Cat a careless lick or two to wring out another ounce of supper, and moved away from the bucket. Cat continued to lap up the milk that remained in the creases at the bucket's bottom; then, still in the bucket, she began cleaning her fur.

The entire incident unfolded so quickly that I decided to remain a spectator. Finally, I emptied the bucket of Cat. None the worse for her adventure, she continued to clean herself in the grass near the pasture gate.

Returning to the house to get a second bucket of milk for the pigs, I related the latest Cat n' Calf episode to Stella who followed me outside, laughing. As I walked toward the pig pen, Stella yelled, pointing toward the gate. Cat had fearlessly rolled over near Calf's hind legs and had begun shadow boxing Calf's tail—or maybe, in Cat's overly active imagination, it was an invisible foe coming in for an aerial attack on poor Calf.

SCHOOL WEEKENDS

How quickly my summer had passed on the farm. All too soon, I was back home immersed in the humdrum of Pittsburgh and small town Sheraden. There were daily newspapers to deliver, school to attend, homework to be completed—all the necessary stuff that caused youth to die a little more each day.

After the summer on the farm, I felt that I had lived too much, too soon.

One day in October, about mid-week, I received a call from Stella. Would I like to come out Saturdays to do chores while she and Merle went to the Southside Farmers' Market, she asked.

I couldn't keep the smile off of my face all that evening. Home duties and school assignments were completed in record time. Nothing could stand in the way of my Friday afternoon departures to Washington County.

SHORTCUT

During the late fall, chores on the farms slowed to daily cow milking and egg collection. Early each Saturday morning, Merle and Stella drove the truck loaded with farm produce to the farmer's market in South Side Pittsburgh, where they would spend the day. My job was to clean the chicken coop. The task was typically a half-day's work and I earned $2.50 for the effort. Much of the $2,50 went for round-trip bus fare. But the escape and the anticipation of adventure made every minute worth the investment.

On weekends back in Pittsburgh, cousin, Mike, or older brother, Norm, delivered my paper route. By 5:30 p.m. each Friday, I was on a Greyhound bus heading south into Washington County.

As the days became shorter, I walked from the McMurray bus stop to the farm in the semi-darkness. The trip was either a longer hike by road, or a cross-country shortcut across Dutch's farm. I carried a Boy Scout flashlight in order to find the spot to climb over the electric fence. As dark descended, the hike became dangerous.

The blacktop was a narrow two-laner. By walking on the right shoulder, I could avoid some of the blinding glare from oncoming headlights. The hill, where the highway turned to circle Dutch's pasture, could easily be spotted on the darkest night since car lights would appear from behind the curve. It was a welcome sight after a long, scary walk.

On one hike, the flashlight dimmed until the filament was a tiny pinpoint of light incapable of lighting up a face in a dark closet. I was never able to find a set of those "super, long lasting" batteries as advertised in *Boy's Life* and on the back covers of comic books. Maybe the advertisements were a bit exaggerated when they promised light all night. On the other hand, I bought fresh batteries only once a season. With travel and newspaper delivery expenses, I could easily rationalize taking a chance—or hoping for moonlit nights for walking.

During the night of the failing flashlight, I walked the blacktop safely the distance to the Dutch's farm shortcut. I climbed under the electric fence and into the pasture feeling secure. Dutch's farm was directly over the hill in a straight line. A few hundred yards of darkness to the top of the hill and there would be farm light the rest of the way to Merle's.

The flashlight turned out to be almost useless. It was starting to rain. The night had become miserable.

Suddenly, my body pitched forward. Hands felt hair as a prostrate cow emitted a strange deep-throated moan. The flashlight hit the ground and rolled downhill. In the pitch blackness, the tiny light looked like a firefly with a short circuit. The flashlight flipped over and over, out of sight.

I struggled to get up and fell again. It's impossible to imagine how large a cow is until you try to climb over one in the dark. My imagination was running wild. Could this be a bull? Dogs and cats can see at night, why not bulls? Would it come after me—or worse yet, get up with me astride its back?

The body shifted. Looking back on the incident, I suspect the cow breathed a bored sigh. But there I was, convinced that this huge animal was a bull. To return to the road in the dark without the flashlight was out of the question. The electric fence might electrocute me in the rain. My only escape was up-hill.

Monkey style, hands and legs took on a will of their own as one-hundred-yard uphill records were broken that evening. At that moment, had I tripped over another cow, my body would have fallen lifeless to the wet ground. It would lie there in the wet grass in the cold and dark all night. They'd find me the next day and mourn the loss.

Farm lights were a welcome sight. With a mixture of joy and relief, I staggered on down the hill, through the fence gate, and onto Dutch's patio. Will had gone to bed early. I explained the incident to his mother.

"Well, we're glad you're okay," she suddenly responded, as though her mind was somewhere else. I felt awkward.

Her face suddenly sparked to life with a maternal smile.

"I'll tell Will that you stopped by," she assured me. The door closed, as she disappeared back into the kitchen.

Sitting on the stone wall near Will's patio, my body continued to shake from the incident. My gaze wandered down the valley toward Merle's. I could just discern his electric fence as it reflected Will's patio light. Collecting my jacket, I continued through a misty rain to Merle's.

The next day, while Merle and Stella were at market, I conducted a search for the flashlight and came up empty. The Boy Scout flashlight is still out there, somewhere on Dutch's hill.

BOW HUNTING

For several weeks during the late fall, I planned my bow-hunting expedition on Merle and Stella's farm. I bought a cheap straight-limb bow at Rizik's Discount Emporium, near my home in Pittsburgh. It was a bow like the ones used in the Robin Hood movies, not a fancy recurve bow like hunters use today. If Robin Hood could get uncanny accuracy, shooting an arrow through a tiny tree knot at 50 paces with his straight-limb bow, then I could surely hit a rabbit with mine. I also bought two target arrows.

The plan was simple enough: hunt for rabbits or anything else that flew, crawled or tried to run. A dollar for the round-trip bus fare and $3 for the bow and arrows demanded that I return with something to show for my investment.

Merle understood my thinking well enough. He said that if I didn't kill anything, I could still clean the chicken coop and earn $2.50 while he and Stella spent the day at the farmers' market in South Side Pittsburgh. Merle was being tactful because I was there to work, not to try out my bow hunting skills.

That November morning, Washington County was breezy and cold. Leaves lay on the ground. Winter bird songs, the cawing of crows, an occasionally a pheasant squawk were all that I heard in the crisp winter air. The birds will be targets, too, I thought, as I shivered my way to the chicken coops.

Cleaning a chicken coop was a solid two-hour job of scraping and collecting droppings and old hay, then depositing fresh hay on the floor. I scraped and cleaned up what seemed like hundreds of pounds of frozen droppings. The job didn't warm me up that biting cold day.

Finally, I headed for the fields beyond the pasture determined to try my new bow. Within 30 minutes, the cold had penetrated through coat and gloves. Then I spotted the rabbit.

Busily chewing, he sat near an oak with his back toward me. There were no dried leaves to warn him of my advance, but I had to get much closer or chance missing with the arrow.

In the Robin Hood movies, I remembered that archers would steady their aim against a tree. Out of the corner of my eye, I saw a large tree. At least it would shield me from the biting wind. The rabbit jumped a short nervous hop, then another. I moved toward the oak with the hop, guessing that he would not see my motion. The rabbit was still facing away and continued his chewing.

I stopped and began to lean slowly toward the tree, not daring to move my feet. The tree suddenly seemed farther away. My left shoulder banged hard against the rough bark. I concentrated on not crying out.

From my clumsy position, I pulled the bow string taut against my cheek. My fingers had held the arrow at the ready for the last half-hour and my glove had frozen to the string. The glove tore from my hand and continued a short distance toward the rabbit. I lost sight of the arrow, which obviously missed its mark. The glove fell quietly to the grass.

I reached slowly for my last arrow. With cold, bare fingers, I again took aim. As the arrow released, the rabbit hopped. The arrow hit the ground directly behind him. The rabbit took another hop. His front legs pawed the air. He did not advance from the spot. Then he moved about a foot, then another, dragging the arrow behind. Could I have pinned it through the tail? That's impossible, I thought. But my arrow disappeared into the underbrush.

I lost the rabbit in tall grass near some bramble. All became still. There I was, unable to locate my first arrow and the rabbit had stolen my last arrow. I recovered my glove and returned to the farm, chilled and shaking.

Later, I related the incident to Merle. He said little, but walked across the kitchen and into the cold storage room. A short time later, he emerged red-faced, faking a cough.

Bow hunting didn't appeal to me after that. I left the bow at the farm, determined never again to give Merle a reason to laugh at me.

EGG HUNTER

One unusually warm November Saturday, Stella and Merle decided not to go to the farmer's market.

Following early morning milking, animal feeding, egg collection, and breakfast, I joined Merle on the porch. He had brought two of his 22-caliber rifles down from the upstairs gun cabinet and was holding a box of fifty shells in his hand.

"Something to do till lunch," he winked.

Old Mitzi, Merle's beagle, was standing there wagging her tail when she spotted something near Dutch's fence and began her slow limp down the driveway toward Venetia Road. Before her arthritis had set in, she was the best pheasant flusher around Washington County. Now, she'd walk and stop, walk and stop. The arthritis was in her hips.

Merle called it egg-hunting—shooting eggs on fence posts located across the farm yard from the front porch. I had his old Stevens break-apart, single-shot 22 rifle. Maybe the aim was off. I kept missing the eggs.

Suddenly, I noticed a momentary shift in the wheat grass beyond; first a movement, and then stillness. I knew that a rabbit would do that—come to a dead stop to listen for the slightest sound.

Adjusting my aim, I eased off a shot into the tall grass. With a hunter's satisfaction, I watched a sudden lurch, then an off-white blur as the animal—not a rabbit at all—jumped for the last time.

"Mitzi!" I screamed, running, throwing the rifle to the ground. Her glassy eyes were unblinking. I stooped and gently touched her.

I think of Mitzi even now and the terrible sadness and remorse well up, sticking in my throat.

TICKER'S COMPROMISE

When I was growing up in Pittsburgh, it seemed that every kid had a dog. Many of us had some good dog stories. More than once I told one about a terrier named Ticker.

Early one Saturday evening, I walked across the pasture to visit Will, a 16-year old farm neighbor. Will's house sat well up on a hill of knee-high grass, above the reddog road.

Will was proud of his terrier's ability to flush pheasants, despite her size. Every time Will mentioned her name in the conversation, Ticker's eyes and ears instantly focused forward, as though awaiting his command.

Ticker was an unusual terrier with a dark, almost-black coat. The only survivor of a winter birth that killed the mother and the rest of the litter, Ticker was intelligent, affectionate and devoted to Will.

That evening was my first experience with Ticker's brand of pheasant flushing. Will, eager to show me Ticker's art, called out, "Flush, Ticker, flush!"

Ticker soared off the porch and into the tall grass. She disappeared immediately as though the grass had taken a tiny gulp. I laughed, thinking of the impossibility of this little dog's task.

But Ticker's entire head and shoulders reappeared. She leapt forward, pressing her front paws down against the grass. At great speed, she repeated the process over and over again. She serpentined across the wide field, continuing her ballet-like leaps.

I saw a pheasant then, its long tail brushing the grass, bright feathers flashing, wings motorized to a frenzy to flee from Ticker's aggressive advance. The show was pure beauty. I was overwhelmed by Ticker's instinct and Will's training. Will clicked an imaginary gun, pretending to shoot the pheasant out of the air.

The next instant, something happened that would have farmers talking for some time. A shadow stirred in a dark corner of the pasture, near the road. Ticker approached the spot quickly.

In the evening light, it was difficult to identify just what it was, but something rose straight up from the grass on tremendous dark wings. Ticker must have figured it was just another pheasant. Everything was bigger than she was. She pursued.

Perhaps it was an eagle or a large hawk. Just above the grass, it turned and attacked. Then the bird either fell to one side or simply lost its grip on Ticker. Maybe Ticker reverted to her rat-terrier instincts and snapped at the bird. The thing ran for several feet, wings beating down the grass, following Ticker's retreat toward the house.

Once airborne, the large bird slowly arced across the road into the woods beyond. Will was shaken. Ticker was suddenly in Will's arms, trembling but unharmed.

Will coaxed Ticker for several days, but the dog wouldn't flush pheasants. She had completely lost the desire. Will was heartbroken.

Later on, I visited Ticker and Will. Will was his old self, obviously recovered from the mishap.

"I want to show you Ticker's latest trick," he exclaimed. "I call this trick 'Ticker's Compromise.' Watch!"

Will suddenly gave the command, "Ticker! Flush, girl, flush!" Ticker bounded into the grass. I was stunned.

A pheasant rose near a clump of snake grass, wings chopping at the air, grabbing for altitude. I was once more entranced by the dog's spirit and skill.

Will laughed, "Keep an eye on the fence down by the road, where that bird attacked her."

Ticker's pattern suddenly changed. In a wide, skirting motion, she avoided an entire acre along the dark corner. Then, the rest of her task completed, she made a beeline toward the patio and jumped into Will's outstretched arms.

FRAN

My sojourn on the farm would not have been nearly as interesting without Fran. I have never forgotten her, and still treasure a laminated photo of Fran, mounted astride her black and tan wonder horse, Buddy.

To this day, I keep the picture in my old western-engraved rawhide wallet, the one I used when I worked on the farm. I've thought of Fran often, and wondered what life had dealt this friend of mine.

I remember her pleasant way; the long talks each day, and a feeling that she wanted to see me tomorrow.

We'd walk into the pasture to entice shy Buddy. To what lengths we'd go to catch that old horse, saddle him and ride double till sunset. They were such adventures then.

Her father explained the warm feel of infected grain. Fran said, "Let's go check to make sure." We walked to the barn and reached deep into one container filled with grain. It was warm. Her dad was not nearly as pleased as we were with our discovery.

I remember an evening we were alone in the house—the hail and thunder. Scared, Fran put her arm across my shoulder. Her face brushed my cheek and we kissed.

127

WINTER MAIL

It had snowed all day and night and most of the following day. Rural mail delivery hadn't been through for two days. The fall of pelting, wet snow had laid a blanket far up the fence posts. Pastures were unfit for grazing. Cattle were brought into barns. Electric fences were turned off. When this had happened before, my friend Fran would go to pick up the mail and deliver it on horseback.

Some adjoining farms covered several hundred acres and were spaced far apart. Buddy, Fran's horse, could trot the main road blindfolded but Fran, who had a detailed knowledge of the area, would chance cross-country riding to save time. She knew the shortcuts, and where the pasture gates were located that led to the farm houses. What Fran and Buddy didn't know was that the landscape held a dangerous alteration.

Down on the O'Brian farm, Bill O'Brian's sons had expanded the grazing area for some of the young bulls. New barbed wire was being installed. Buddy ran into some, reared, and became entangled in the wire mesh. The sudden captivity and pain from the barbs frightened Buddy causing him to rear again and again. After some effort, Fran was able to turn the horse around with a maneuver that probably saved its life. But the fore-belly and front legs were badly torn.

That evening, several of us visited Fran and Buddy at the barn. She related her desperate attempt to get Buddy home before dark, and before shock set in from loss of blood, a trail of which ran for a half-mile along the reddog road.

Buddy lay on his side in a stall. A local vet had trudged cross-country earlier, and was there when we arrived. The tendons had not been damaged. Buddy would be fine by spring.

The following morning, I walked to the O'Brian's farm. The snow had melted some, but the fence and surrounding area reflected all too clearly Fran's and Buddy's terrible struggle. Pieces of flesh and hair clung to the barbs of wire. Crimson splashes puddled near the fence in the wet snow. I found blood specks in a three-hundred square foot circle, evidence of Fran's determined efforts to turn the bolting, frightened horse.

In subsequent storms, no one volunteered to deliver rural mail on horseback.

130

HUNTING SEASON

Many stories circulated among the farmers about the damage that naïve or malicious hunters do to farm property and to both wild and domestic animals. Stella had told me that it was not unusual to find shot embedded in the sides of the house after the hunting season. By the time fall hunting season began in Washington County, I was as apprehensive as everyone else.

One Saturday, during the shortening daylight of late fall, I was, as usual, alone at the farm. Jim had long since moved to the Raccoon State Park area to attempt strawberry farming with his family. Merle and Stella were at the farmers' market all day.

"Tell them anything, but don't let them hunt on the property," Merle coached as he and Stella climbed into the truck loaded for market somewhat earlier. "Dogs, chickens,

I've even seen cows shot by some of these city hunters. Sometimes it's out of spite. They're getting even for being turned away. Hell, they even skinned a cow on one farm near here."

"You've got to be courteous, but firm," Merle yelled to me from the truck, as he drifted it out toward the road in low gear for an easy start.

Worried by Merle's words, I strapped on his pistol when I answered a hunter's knock at the door later that day. Black pistol belt, black holster, and a black revolver, strapped to a husky, young, tan-faced farm boy.

"Do you mind if we hunt at the back of your property for a few hours?" a tall, friendly gentleman inquired. He was probably an engineer or a lawyer who went out to the country one day a year—and this was it, I thought to myself.

"Well, you would have more success across the road, on the hill," I said. "That's where I hunt small game. There are a lot of pheasants in that field. They come from the woods surrounding the well rigging, near the top there." I came out on the porch facing his friends.

One of the hunters had his gun accidentally pointed at the other. Trying not to notice, I raised my arm and motioned to my right across the reddog road, making sure they saw the sidearm.

"Hey, thanks a lot. We really appreciate it." The tall one joined his friends. Their large, new boots scuffed down the driveway announcing themselves to the echoing hillsides. How they expected to shoot anything but a blind, deaf animal, I didn't know.

But they had seen Merle's pistol on my hip. There would be no shenanigans on Merle's property from this group.

I waved and smiled what I considered a reassuring smile to the hunters and walked back into the house, letting the screen and main door slam with some authority. I heard them chattering like they were going on a camp-out rather than to stalk wild, cunning, and evasive animals.

"One shot and every animal in Washington County will run onto the game refuge," I mumbled aloud, laughing to myself.

The chicken coop had to be cleaned soon, I thought. That was my only real chore and justified my trip from home to the country each weekend during the school year. Chicken coop cleaning was more of an obstacle than a chore. I didn't savor the thought of scraping up frozen droppings which had accumulated for two weeks on the coop floor. Along fifty or more running feet of roosts, the chickens graciously deposited droppings to a three or four-inch depth. In the winter, the droppings became a hardened mortar-like substance mixed generously with an ammonia smell. What took one hour's cleaning in the summer became a back-breaking, thankless two-hour job in the cold of late fall and winter. If the job wasn't done properly, the droppings would harden to the feet of the chickens.

I couldn't answer doors and clean coops at the same time, I rationalized, so I went upstairs to await further knocks at the door. Daylight would be around a few more hours and Merle and Stella wouldn't be back until after sunset. Lying on the bed, I let my gaze wander through the window to the haystack beyond the chicken yard, where we often did our target shooting with rifles. I couldn't pass up the chance. Getting up, I placed the pistol barrel across the sill and under the bottom of the raised window, pointing it out across the back yard. The window-opening left just enough extra room to aim down the sights. That would take care of the gun bucking in my hand and the bullet going through the roof or something.

My finger eased down on the trigger as I stopped breathing for just a moment. The report from the revolver was a mind-numbing explosion. The house vibrated with the discharge; then quiet descended like darkness. I could hear ringing in my ears and little else. Maybe my head shouldn't have been so close to the gun's barrel when it discharged. With some satisfaction, I saw that the window had stopped the upward movement of the gun, but the barrel had skewed to the right a bit, toward the chicken yard.

Suddenly tired, I holstered the gun, removed the gun belt, placed them in Merle's room in his gun cabinet, and then lay down on the bed again.

When I woke, the sun had set. Evening was quickly becoming night. The chicken coop hadn't been cleaned. I raced out of the house and up to the coop.

The chickens had returned from the chicken yard and were quieting down for the night. Some were already on the roosts.

In an hour the coop was finished—well, sort of finished. Quickly, I deposited fresh straw over the bare floor, fed the chickens and went to turn off the coop's lights. Something in the chicken yard caught my eye. At first, it looked like a large splash of white paint.

"Who would spill white paint in the chicken…" my words trailed off. The paint spot was a dead chicken. Closer inspection proved that the chicken had been shot.

"My God, I shot a chicken!" The words rolled off my tongue just as a truck slowed at the driveway. I picked up the dead chicken, ran to the back of the coop where I knew boards were missing, and pitched the dead carcass as hard and as far under the coop as I could. Arriving at the front of the farm house, I greeted Merle and Stella as they parked in the driveway.

"Well, young fella, any hunters stop by?" Merle's voice sounded the slightest bit apprehensive.

"Yes, Merle, earlier today. I noticed someone walk behind the chicken coop. There were three hunters. Said they were looking for someone to give them permission to hunt at the back of the property. Well, I directed them across the road. Told them how good the small game hunting was in that field up by the well rigging. They almost seemed too friendly, though—couldn't figure it out."

The lie poured out smoothly.

"One of those guys was actually pointing his gun at the other one. Can you believe that, Merle? And none of them even knew it—you know, hunter safety." Finally, I shut up and began to unload the truck.

Later, we ate supper and Merle offered to drive me to McMurray to catch the early evening Greyhound for Pittsburgh.

Toward the middle of the following week, Stella called on the phone.

"Your friend Murphy and his brother came out Sunday to hunt. Since Merle won't need your help for the remaining winter months, I packed up your clothes and the boys took them to Pittsburgh to save you the trip."

Somewhere, deep inside, a tiny voice said, "You've been found out." I thanked Stella for her thoughtfulness.

It would be the next summer before I would visit the farm once again.

AFTERWARDS...

Courtesy of Wally & Bonnie Gerhold
Ray and Merle Gerhold
Brothers, farm owners and neighbors

THE FOLLOWING SUMMER

The following summer I returned to the farm with older brother, Norm. I was curious about my old friends and was anxious to share their farm stories with him. First, we stopped at Fran's. But Fran had left for the summer to visit a favorite aunt in New England -- a high school graduation gift from her parents. The old horse Buddy appraised me as though we'd never been introduced.

139

Norm and I continued up the reddog to the front of Ray's farm. Merle, big as last summer, was hunched down at the farm entrance, forcing grease into a wheel bearing on a hay wagon. He started to ramble on about war, cursing all the death. Each time he blew smoke from his Lucky Strike, he looked up with a quick glance before returning his attention to his work.

My long held apprehensions surfaced once again. Maybe Merle had discovered the dead chicken I accidentally shot and had thrown under the coop the previous fall. Maybe he had discovered that I had shot every gun he owned at least once—he had a bunch—and I hadn't cleaned them to cover my tracks. My guilty conscience forced me to go through an old check-list of other farm antics and connivery from the previous year.

Later, Norm commented that Merle was trying to scare us with all the blood and guts tales. But I felt that he was subtly conveying a far more serious message.

We said our goodbyes and continued down the reddog road. Little Wally wasn't to be seen. With the cold reception from Merle, I decided not to yell back and ask him where Wally was hiding. Norm and I decided to shortcut through Dutch's farm on our way back to the bus, stopping to visit with Will. His mother explained that Will had joined the Army. She appeared sad and pensive. I learned later that Jim had joined the Army as well.

Ticker, Will's pheasant flushing terrier, remembered me like yesterday. He demonstrated a few unsolicited tricks. I showed Norm the tiny dog's skill at flushing pheasants.

Wonderful little Ticker revived many of the memories from that previous summer.

Will's mother, and Norm and I sat and talked for some time, relating country stories and happenings from previous visits. She probably missed Will and was glad for young company. We graciously accepted her "picked pie" and home-made ice cream. Norm and I knew all about picked pie and told her about our mother, aunts, and their friends back home, going on all-day berry picking expeditions at our Uncle John's farm.

As we ate, Will's mother explained that the picked pie tradition went back generations to early America, the wagon trains of the 1800's, the Oregon pioneers of the early 1900's, and the long-standing traditions of both farm and city families across the country. She was suddenly a storehouse of knowledge.

Will's mother was immediately memorialized in the Mom Hall of Fame when she produced a bag of home-made cookies for consumption during the long walk back to the McMurray bus stop. Norm and I continued to carry on our conversation with her, laughing and waving as we departed on the walk up Dutch's hill, the memorable short-cut to reach the highway on the other side.

Ticker accompanied us to the top of the hill. Norm and I decided to search for the Boy Scout flashlight I had lost the previous fall. Back then, the pasture was a dark, wet, foreboding cow-ridden hill. The flashlight was waterproof and would probably still work fine.

Ticker hung around for a few minutes, realized that no further petting or praise was forthcoming, politely wagged goodbye and darted back toward Will's patio. We hunted for the flashlight until we had eaten all the cookies. The decision was made to continue to the bus stop.

During that final few-mile hike, I related stories to Norm— many since forgotten—about the farms along the way.

We caught the 3:00 p.m. bus back to Pittsburgh. This visit to the farm would be my final taste of country livin' and my last visit as a teenager.

MORE RECENTLY

Years later I learned that Jim and Will joined the Army. Jim participated in the Pan Olympics as an Army heavyweight boxer. After his Army service ended, Jim found work as a lineman for a Nevada power company, and worked his way into management. He now considers himself "retired" in Oregon.

For some reason, I can't picture Jim hitting a ball around a golf course for very long. No, I think life holds a lot more in store for him.

After the Army, Will married, raised a family, and now oversees the family's third generation Farm Market in Washington County.

Fran has five grown children and lives near Canonsburg. Her family's farm was sold and parceled into mini-estates—

one estate is located directly across the reddog (since paved) from Merle and Stella's farm.

Little Wally, now "big" Wally, and his wife, Bonnie, continue to run his father's (Merle's brother, Ray's) farm.

Wally maintains a completely operational farm.

For many years, Wally also held a position with a utility company, while continuing to work the farm.

Courtesy of Wally & Bonnie Gerhold
Wally, at nine, on his Dad's (Ray's) Farmall F-20

Courtesy of Wally & Bonnie Gerhold
Recently: Wally at the barn, holding two newborn Piglets

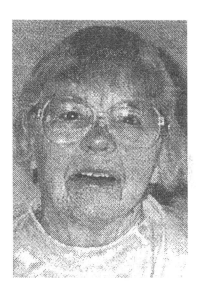

STELLA REVISITED

In the Fall of 1996, I visited Wally's and Bonnie's home on a trip to Pittsburgh from Northern Virginia. Wally was out in the fields doing some last minute mowing before an anticipated cold, stormy night. We visited briefly with Bonnie, then, before it became too dark, drove the half-mile down Venetia road (renamed: Justa Bout Road) to visit with Stella.

I had made a phone call to Merle the previous fall. He was not feeling well.

145

"If I can make it to next summer, I might be OK," Merle said. Merle passed away the following April.

During that fall phone conversation, Merle managed to add a few more farm stories of his own. One he recalled was a rope climbing episode at the barn during my second day at the farm. Climbing a rope was something Merle and I could do with relative ease, but poor lanky, long armed Jim, couldn't climb more than a few feet without sinking back to the ground.

When Jim was around, Merle and I would demonstrate our ability to rope climb, up to the loading gates on the second floor, above the barn entrance. We're not sure if Jim ever forgave us.

Stella mentioned that she was content to remain on the farm where she and Merle had spent their entire married lives. She said her nephew Wally and wife, Bonnie, visited daily with hot meals and to provide the latest farm news.

Walking outside Merle and Stella's house, I noticed a relatively barren field between the back of the house and the old Chicken yard, some hundred feet away. Years earlier, a small vegetable garden and peach orchard dominated the area.

I heard no chicken sounds and decided that most of them had been taken to market long ago. True to Merle's love of dogs, an old hound was tied up to a dog house, next to the farm house.

Stella commented sadly about the big, new houses being built in the area, one located across the road. It was on an acre or so of the old Johnston farm property that bordered the road. Stella couldn't understand why people needed such large homes.

Beyond the new house, up on the hill I spotted the power lines, where, so many years earlier, I had sent several hunters to get them off Merle's property. An old oil rig had disappeared. During my stay on the farm, an oil drilling company had drilled many thousands of feet into the earth and found nothing. They had left the old rig behind.

Yet, Stella agrees, though the farms have diminished in number, little else has changed over the years in the farming communities of Washington County, Pennsylvania. But then, you don't want to mess with perfection.

Andrew Stevans

ACKNOWLEDGEMENTS

Without my friend, Jim, and the farm folk mentioned herein, there would be no farm stories. As an aside, it's unfortunate the farm families did not take many photos over the years. Bonnie, Wally's wife, was able to find several, some of poor quality due to age. For these reasons I decided to offer the following summary.

MERLE was Jim and my farm employer many years earlier. He passed away quietly in April, 1996. In earlier years a tractor had rolled over Merle and he lived to tell about it.

I was fortunate to speak with Merle by phone in the fall of 1995. He assured me that he had led a full and happy life. "I want to make it to next summer and the warm days," he had said. I sent Merle and Stella some of the farm stories from COUNTRY LIVIN' before they appeared in the Sunday Metro section of the Pittsburgh Post Gazette.

To the end, Merle's mind was sharp, his recall uncanny. He shared anecdotes long forgotten by Jim and me, incidents that happened during our working that summer on his farm.

During the last talk with Merle by phone, without bringing up the subject, I concluded he had forgiven me for shooting each of his guns at least once while he and Stella were at the Southside Farmers' Market those many years ago (*Hunting Season*). I didn't ask Merle if he had found the dead chicken I accidentally shot and threw under the chicken house back then, nor did I broach the subject of the poorly cleaned chicken house.

Stella said Merle and their farm friends and family were delighted to read the farm stories and see Merle's and Stella's names in the Pittsburgh Post Gazette during March and early April of 1996, before Merle's passing. Three of the published farm stories that Merle found joy in reading were: *"Washington County," "Neutralizing Connie,"* "and *"Red's Best Shot."*

STELLA was a second mother to us boys. She was strict but accepting of our teen age shenanigans. Back then, Jim's or my mother spoke with Stella occasionally on the phone. I'm pretty sure it was to check up on their sons' misadventures as much as anything else. All Jim and I heard was, "your mother called, we had a nice conversation…"

Stella and Merle kept two see-through glass jars full of Orange Slices, those gelatin and sugar delicacies that Jim savored almost as much as I did. The other jar contained Circus Peanuts, *"orange in color, banana in flavor, and peanut in design,"* as the advertising claimed. The Circus Peanuts were my favorite, but both candies were there for the taking. I'm sure they contained some essential nutrients for us growing teens.

Stella was far beyond most people with her vast knowledge of insect larvae, butterfly and moth species. Her and her dad's collection of moths is on display at the Carnegie museum in Pittsburgh. I'm told her love of flowers rivaled her knowledge of the insect kingdom.

But, before all else, Stella and Merle were dedicated to each other and to running their farm together.

RAY, Merle's brother, owned the farm adjacent to Merle's farm, and was supportive of everything Merle did. They were close brothers, joined by their love of farm-life. Back in the day, I considered Ray a friend that I could rely on if I needed advice or help when Merle and Stella were at the Southside Farmers' market.

Ray owned a somewhat larger farm than Merle's 40 acres. Both he and Merle belonged to a farm cooperative. During harvesting season, the farms shared harvesting equipment and the work load. Jim and I were fortunate to be included in this co-op group and to share in the story telling and camaraderie. We can never forget and lunch feasts that the farm wives prepared for the entire field crew each day of harvesting.

WALLY has managed his dad, Ray's farm for many years. Bonnie, Wally's wife and he are dedicated farm folk. But Wally also has worked full-time at a local utility company. Stella mentioned that they both cared for her daily, following Merle's passing.

It has to be strenuous to hold a full-time job and also do planting and harvesting of winter and summer wheat and oats. This effort, combined with the daily care of pigs, cows and chickens over many years puts Wally in the farming Hall of Fame. Wally's heart has always been "on the farm."

The stories, *"Wally Rider"* and *"Pig Orchard"* were selected among the best dozen stories in readings by several Virginia junior and senior high schools and by students at the junior college level. COUNTRY LIVIN' was selected over related books by these same students.

Thank you Wally and Bonnie for being there during the final drafts of the book, and for supplying old photos and related commentary on your families, and on the farms of Washington County.

JIM was a friend of my eldest brother during their grade school years. Our parents were friends as well. Often, during those unforgettable years, we boys and dad, Jim and his older brother, George, and several other families enjoyed playing softball games each summer in the field behind our house. The desire to win was always there, but the camaraderie always seemed to come first.

That pretty well says it all in regard to Jim's and my association over the years. We had more than a few similar experiences during our formative years, particularly while attending the Catholic grade school under the sharp eyes of the Sisters of Charity. We played a number of pick-up touch football games with Jim, my two brothers, and several neighbor friends, taking on all who challenged us. But, I can never forget working that memorable summer on the farm, before Jim's family moved to their own farm-- *"Jim's Departure"*--in COUNTRY LIVIN'.

After his time in the U.S. Army, Jim married and moved to Reno, Nevada. I served in the U.S. Navy, married, and moved to Fairfax, Virginia. Our paths did not cross for many years.

Jim and I had been in touch by phone during Merle's last days, but it was a pleasant coincidence when Jim's sister, living in Green County, Pennsylvania, called Jim to mention that she was reading the COUNTRY LIVIN' stories running, off and on, for over a year in the Sunday Pittsburgh Post Gazette. Shortly afterwards, Jim and I were both surprised to learn that the farm families had read our farm adventures. We both got that old feeling of close family and friends, and re-experienced the exhilaration we had while working together on the farm.

By Andrew Stevans...

ATLANTIC FLEET
A Navy Man's Sea Stories

COUNTRY LIVIN'
Two City Teens work a Summer on the Farm
(Sub-Title: The Farms of Washington County, PA)

GROWIN' UP
The Way Things Used to be—and Still Ought to be...

PREP SCHOOL DAYS
The Seminary at the University of Notre Dame

THINKING IN PRIVATE
The Past, Present and Future...

155

Made in the USA
Charleston, SC
12 March 2015